The Half-Shilling Curate, as he was affectionately known by his family, tells the very personal story of an Army Chaplain – The Reverend Herbert Butler Cowl – from Christmas Eve 1914 to the end of hostilities in 1919. His descriptive account, from his own personal letters and writings, illustrates the value of faith during the war and the balance between serving God and carrying out his duties as a captain in the British Army.

Herbert's engaging story told of the man who matured from humble Christian beginnings to the start of his journey discovering faith, love and a sense of duty and moral responsibility. At the outbreak of war, he volunteered to become a Wesleyan Army Chaplain. With meticu-lous detail, the reader is taken on Herbert's journey with the Durham Light Infantry from the objective view of life in the Army Home Camp in Aldershot, to the adventure of France and the reality of Flanders on the Western Front near Armentières.

Whilst serving at the front, his service was cut short when he was severely wounded during heavy enemy bombardment at the front. On his journey back to England, he was placed in a cot bed aboard the hospital ship *Anglia* when she hit a German mine in the Channel. As a result of Herbert's actions on that fateful day, he became one of the first Wesleyan Army Chaplains to receive the Military Cross for exemplary gallantry. He was the only known Army Chaplain to be awarded the Military Cross Medal for his action on a ship during the Great War.

His second battle was recovery – and although he was never fit enough to return to overseas duties, he returned to work as an Army Chaplain in the army garrisons and home camps in England. The book gives an insight into day-to-day life and the strains of service as an Army Chaplain on the home front at Colchester and Portsmouth.

Twenty years later, Herbert – a Methodist minister with a family living in Acton – found himself in the centre of another conflict: the Second World War. As he stayed in London through the London Blitz, again the reader gains an understanding of one man's faith during war and the comparisons that can be seen for a new generation.

Herbert's story concludes with the final chapter of his life and the intimate observa-tions of a spiritual man driven to follow his faith in wartime.

Born and educated in Pembrokeshire, Sarah Reay lives in rural Northumberland with her husband and two sons. She began her working life as a horse instructress in the New Forest, relocated to Corsica in order to become a fluent French speaker, worked as a project manager for a property developer in London and now runs a facilities management consultancy with her husband in the North East of England. However, from an early age, her father, Michael Cowl (son of 'The Half-Shilling Curate') encouraged her to nurture an inquisitive interest in history. Those early days of youthful curiosity developed in her a great enthusiasm for the past, especially the Great War. From the thrills of flying a First World War replica bi-plane, to visiting the sombre graves of those fallen in battle, Sarah embarked on years of research in locations across England, France and Belgium to become a dedicated self-taught historian. Sarah's unstinting and unrelenting desire to research meticulously the account of her grandfather's role in the Great War has given her a considerable understanding of Army Chaplaincy. As a Christian, Sarah has become engrossed in her grandfather's unique and intriguing tale of war and faith.

The Half-shilling Curate

A Personal Account of War and Faith 1914–1918

Sarah Reay

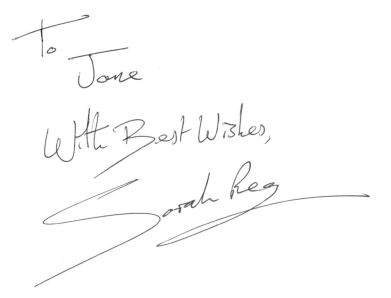

To Jane

With Best Wishes,

Sarah Reay

Helion & Company Limited

Helion & Company Limited
26 Willow Road
Solihull
West Midlands
B91 1UE
England
Tel. 0121 705 3393
Fax 0121 711 4075
Email: info@helion.co.uk
Website: www.helion.co.uk
Twitter: @helionbooks
Visit our blog http://blog.helion.co.uk/

Published by Helion & Company 2016. 2nd edition published 2018
Designed and typeset by Mach 3 Solutions Ltd (www.mach3solutions.co.uk)
Cover designed by Paul Hewitt, Battlefield Design (www.battlefield-design.co.uk)
Printed by Short Run Press, Exeter, Devon

Text © Sarah Reay 2016, 2018
Images © as individually credited
Maps drawn by George Anderson, © Helion & Company 2016

ISBN 978-1-911096-46-7

British Library Cataloguing-in-Publication Data.
A catalogue record for this book is available from the British Library.

For details of other military history titles published by Helion & Company
Limited contact the above address, or visit our website: http://www.helion.co.uk.

We always welcome receiving book proposals from prospective authors.

This book is dedicated
to the memory of over 5,000 men
who volunteered to become
Army Chaplains during the Great War
and to the 179 men who made the ultimate sacrifice,
who did not survive to tell their story.

This is a work of family piety, written with great affection. The letters of the author's grandfather, Rev Herbert Cowl, provide the basis for his biography, focusing on his service as a Wesleyan Army Chaplain in 1915. A wound in November that year ended his short time at the front but the hospital ship on which he was returning from France hit a mine. He escaped his sickbed and threw life rafts to others struggling in the water. Horrific experiences did not diminish his faith and courage; he continued to serve fellow Christians through two world wars. The text is a moving and well-documented story of an admirable family member.

Dr Rodney Atwood, Military Historian

I found the book to be an enthralling and moving experience. You have certainly conveyed your grandfather's deep and compassionate Christian faith, his integrity and nobility of character and his remarkable ability to build up and enlarge the faith of others. His selfless courage and profound humanity are admirably described, and you also summarise his career in the Methodist ministry in a succinct and stimulating fashion. I hope the book will be widely read and appreciated.

Professor John Derry, Historian

This book throws new light on an often overlooked aspect of the war on the Western Front – the chaplaincy service. Men, who are undergoing terrible tribulations in the near-momentary expectation of death or serious injury, have need of spiritual comfort.

This book which is a memoir written by one of the author's forbears brilliantly captures the vital role of Great War chaplains who were striving to give consolation in the midst of the worst war in history, one where weapons of mass destruction really did come of age and brought the randomness of death to countless thousands on a daily basis. Theirs was no easy task and this book brings this facet of war brilliantly to life.

John Sadler, Historian & Author

"The Half-Shilling Curate" tells the story of Herbert Butler Cowl MC, a Wesleyan Army Chaplain of the Great War, through his letters, service record and other contemporary sources and is written by his granddaughter. It is a very well-crafted work, full of interest and worth reading.

Chris Baker, Historian & Author

It is carefully researched and lovingly written. Sarah is fortunate to have many original letters and photographs from Herbert and his family, which makes the narrative come alive. You often feel you are listening in to conversations that took place 100 years ago. At the same time, she has found corroborative evidence from a range of sources, ensuring that this personal story is anchored in the wider historical context and the Wesleyan Church of the era. I found it an easy read, which helped me to glimpse something of the work of those early chaplains. Herbert and many others won much admiration from the serving men for their bravery in being alongside them in the trenches and tending to their practical, pastoral and spiritual needs.

Roger Walton, President of the Methodist Church 2016/2017

He was very evidently the finest of men, and blessed with good looks, and I was most moved by the "love story."

In conclusion, congratulations on bringing such a heart-warming story to light. I did enjoy it – was inspired by it indeed.

Allan Mallinson, Historian & Author

Contents

List of Illustrations

List of Maps

Foreword

The one hundredth anniversary of Great War has meant greater interest in the conflict and the experiences of the generation whose lives were irrevocably changed during those four years. Aspects of the war which have had less attention in previous years have come into sharper focus. One such is the role of chaplains in the armed forces and the stresses and challenges they faced.

Historians in the last couple of years have shed new light on WW1 chaplains, both on how their role evolved and how their experiences in the trenches shaped their ministry when they returned home. Edward Madigan, Peter Howson and Linda Parker are among those who have made valuable contributions in this area. A common theme is how ill-prepared the churches were for the new mass conflict which developed, perhaps reflecting other sections of society. Chaplains had in effect to work out their role for themselves. Some found it easier than others to gain respect and establish credibility with the troops.

My interest was stimulated by the experiences of my grandfather the Rev. Tom Pym DSO. A biography written by my grandmother Dora Pym, "Tom Pym, a Portrait" written in 1952 had sat on a bookshelf only occasionally dipped into. Thanks to a BBC team who knew of my grandfather's story, I was asked to present a piece on WW1 padres and that drew me into the subject.

Tom Pym, it transpired, had been one of a group of chaplains who had insisted on being in or close to the front line trenches. This had been actively discouraged at the start of the war but the military authorities came to realise that chaplains could play an important role in sustaining and encouraging the troops. The commander in chief Sir Douglas Haig, a Scottish Presbyterian, encouraged the padres to roam as they wished in the trenches, noting that "a good chaplain is as valuable as a good general".

Ministering to the men at the front took the padres in harm's way. While they did not bear arms, their courage was severely tested as they came under shellfire or helped gather in the wounded sometimes from No Man's Land. During the course of the war, 179 chaplains died, and there were three Victoria Crosses awarded along with 67 DSOs and 487 MCs.

Geoffrey Studdert-Kennedy, known affectionately as 'Woodbine Willie' for his habit of handing out cigarettes to the troops, and Tubby Clayton and Neville Talbot who co-founded the Toc H rest club in Poperinghe, were among the best known of this new breed of frontline padres. With Tom Pym, and other Anglicans, they looked ahead to how the Church of England might be reformed after the war, shedding its middle class image and becoming more relevant to the lives of working people. Their experience of ministry alongside the Tommies made them realise how out of touch the Church of England had become.

So much for the established church and its concerns, but what of the nonconformists in the Great War? Sarah Reay has provided her own answers to that question with this fascinating book on her grandfather, the Rev. Herbert Cowl M.C. Her coverage of his life before and after the war as well as his wartime experiences gives a compelling account of the Wesleyan Methodist movement. In many ways, it seems, Wesleyans were more in touch with a broad swathe of society than the Church of England. Hence, perhaps, their chaplains found it easier to mix with frontline troops.

But Herbert Cowl's story illustrates how a chaplain's personal qualities were as important as the institution he represented. He notes that some chaplains were content to stay well behind the lines with regimental support staff. But he realised the importance of being close to the men when they were in the firing line and that is why he chose to put himself at risk to fulfil his ministry.

The range of letters and papers left by the Rev. Cowl give far more vivid detail than many other accounts of the life of a wartime padre. He writes extensively and eloquently about his work at the front and the camaraderie with officers and men he served alongside. Sarah Reay has skilfully woven together extracts with the story of his life and times. She has meticulously researched military records to establish his whereabouts and the characters present at important parts of the narrative.

It would be spoiling things to give too much away, but suffice to say that the tale of Herbert Cowl's bravery is a gripping one. There are some moving moments, including the swift arrival of soldiers from the frontline when they heard their chaplain was wounded. His ability to befriend and support the troops in the often appalling conditions they endured led to respect and affection alike. The account of events which resulted in the award of his Military Cross is dramatic to say the least. Herbert Cowl would have been amongst the first chaplain recipients of the Military Cross.

The astonishing story of valour which led to the award might have qualified him for a V.C. if there had been more senior officers present to witness his selfless display of calm and courage in the face of the enemy

Sarah Reay's book also shows how an inner city church minister had to consistently show courage during the Blitz of World War Two. She describes the dangers of everyday life in areas which were heavily bombed. Herbert Cowl's compassion and care of his flock in West London as they struggled to cope with a nightly bombing ordeal come shining through. He and his family's peacetime life on the local Wesleyan circuits is also well documented.

The story of how the Rev. H.B. Cowl lived out his faith under fire is an important addition to our knowledge of chaplaincy in the Great War. His humility, modesty and devotion to others are all too clear along with his trust in God to see him through the most testing of times. Like other padres he would, one suspects, have only felt he was doing his bit and would not have wanted anyone to make a fuss. But it is only right that one hundred years on we recognise their courage and selfless service. If they have not always had the recognition they deserved, then this book helps make amends.

Hugh Pym
London, August 2016

Preface – Who was Herbert?

This is the story of a keen, young, inexperienced Army Chaplain who went to war to serve God, his King and his Country in 1915. He was an ordinary man, a son, brother, uncle, a Wesleyan Methodist minister and my grandfather.

My first recollection of the Rev. Herbert Butler Cowl was at a family tea party in his beautiful secluded wild green garden one afternoon in late summer of 1970 at his home, Newton Cottage, in its remote location on the Isle of Purbeck near Poole in Dorset. My grandmother, Mary had passed away five years earlier, in December 1965 when I was only six months old. The cottage was situated at the end of a very long winding rugged track, nestled amongst the trees and the heath with an open outlook across the estuary towards Brownsea Island. Newton Cottage was enchanting.

I can remember that first memory of Herbert. It was a very warm sunny afternoon and I was staying at Newton Cottage, with my brothers and parents. My grandfather served tea from a quaint old English china tea pot with knitted tea cosy, and all the adults were seated in a tidy fashion drinking from fine bone china teacups and saucers.

Portrait of Herbert taken in Bristol at the end of 1914. (Author's collection)

Homemade cakes and biscuits were served and, as a five-year-old child, I felt it was my duty to my parents to be quiet, to sit still and to wait until I was spoken to. I watched my grandfather quietly entertain the adult members of the family, talking with tenderness, embracing a certain mystery to his voice and gesturing with his waving arms.

'Grandad' was a very old man of average height with a fine bronze-coloured weatherbeaten complexion and a full head of thick snow white hair. His spoken words were delivered in a very mellow peaceful manner. His voice was soft, husky and vibrant with almost an air of magic – I had never heard anyone speak so distinctively before. I learnt later in life that this was due to a piece of German shrapnel that had slashed through his jaw and voice box during a war that had taken place many years before I was born. It turned out that this was also the reason why my grandfather's food had to be chopped and mashed with the back of a fork into small pieces and why he had to chew every mouthful of food more than thirty times. He was a very slow eater.

Two years later, whilst playing at school, in the school playground, I found myself in a position whereby I wanted to trade something for a large collection of green plastic German toy soldier figures in a four litre ice-cream container which one of the schoolboys wanted to sell. Having two elder brothers, I felt that if I had such a big container of toy soldiers, I would have something that they would covet. I didn't have any money so I wondered what I could barter to make a swap. It then occurred to me that I had seen a rather nice medal in the shape of a cross in a smart case, hidden in one of my parents' cupboards. So I took the medal to school and exchanged it for the German soldiers! It was two days later that my father realised what had happened. There was a quick exchange of telephone calls to the school and to the boy's parents – the medal was located and returned to its rightful home. I had to give back the ice-cream container of German soldiers!

It turned out that the medal was actually the Military Cross awarded to my grandfather – this man of gentle and quiet spirit, for an act of exemplary gallantry during the First World War when he had been on board a sinking ship in the English Channel; courageous and determined, he had saved many lives and whilst in the sea he had given his life jacket to someone in the water who he believed needed it more than himself in order to survive.

In 1971 Herbert died from leukaemia aged 85. At this point and for many years that followed, I knew very little of my grandfather and his experiences in World War One.

Now, one hundred years have passed since the beginning of the Great War and whilst looking through some old family papers, I came across a bundle of old letters tucked away and unmentioned for almost a century that Herbert had written to his parents after arrival on the Western Front. The letters continued through to his time spent in the front line trenches of Flanders; a fledgling Army Chaplain ready to follow his path of destiny for God as a Wesleyan minister. These letters inspired me to look further and to find out more about the man who enlisted on Christmas Eve 1914: to discover his journey; who he was; where he was; who he was with; to learn of the places he passed through on his journey through France and Flanders and to see the change from anticipation and excitement to realisation and understanding the terrible cost of the First World War. I was to learn how his faith kept him strong, how he inspired others, how he prepared soldiers for their worst fate, many did not survive and how he comforted the wounded and dying, who did return. One evening in Flanders there was a very heated debate in the officers' mess. Of this, Herbert wrote to his parents:

A doctor in the mess had said, "he had never been near enough to a parson to touch him with a barge pole before". However, at the end of the altercation, "the doctor rose to his feet with angry flush, and as he left he said, "I don't care what you fellows say; but the chap who has got religion is a damned lucky chap"!'

My mother, who is now in her late eighties and my late father, Michael Cowl told me that Herbert never spoke of the war; only that he served alongside the Durham Light Infantry. With the recent discovery of Herbert's letters, writings, photographs and recordings, I have been able to piece together his story; the story of a young Army Chaplain during the Great War. These records relating to the family's history had been kept in boxes and chests by my great grandparents, my grandparents and latterly by my late father. They had been passed down through the generations of the Cowl family and left untouched for nearly a century. Through these letters, writings and photographs, I felt strangely drawn and connected to the past.

With the additional discovery of service records, battalion diaries and church records relating directly to my grandfather's wartime service, I have come to realise that Herbert's story should be heard and understood today and shared with future

Herbert Cowl with his granddaughter, author, Sarah Reay (nee Cowl) in 1965. He was amused by his granddaughter, because when she cried, he thought, her voice resembled that of Sarah Bernhardt, the famous French stage and early film actress who had entertained the French troops during the Great War. (Author's collection)

generations. The personal accounts by Army Chaplains during the Great War have faded and are almost forgotten. This is an account from what is nearly a lost generation – we should remember them.

As a result of my research I have come face to face with my grandfather, learnt of his powerful aura that has come to life through his writing and the memories of others. I have even gained an untouchable sense that he has given me eternal inspiration to write his story. All I had was the memory of a much loved grandfather in his magical kingdom with God, nature and his eclectic collection of books. These precious memories have now been saved for future generations and this story will help others understand a little more about the power of faith during war.

This is the Rev. Herbert Butler Cowl M.C.'s story; Herbert's story; my grandfather's story, 'The Half Shilling Curate''s story!

1

In the Beginning

Herbert Butler Cowl, the son of a highly regarded distinguished Wesleyan Methodist minister, Frederick Bond Cowl was born at The Manse in Headingley, Leeds, on 13 September 1886. Frederick and his wife Mary Ellen both came from large strong middle class Methodist families.

Frederick Cowl was the eighth of sixteen children, the son of a solicitor in Great Yarmouth, Norfolk. After receiving an education at Great Yarmouth Grammar School, Frederick trained and qualified as a solicitor but it was not long afterwards that he decided that his true calling was to the Wesleyan Church and he entered the ministry in 1877. During his early days in the church he met Mary Ellen Butler, a farmer's daughter from the village of Bowerchalke in Wiltshire and also the eldest sister of Frederick's dear friend, the Rev. Herbert William Henry Butler. Mary Ellen was born and brought up in a devout Wesleyan home with two of her brothers entering the ministry. It was not long before love blossomed for Frederick and Mary Ellen and in 1881 they were married at the Butler family's Wesleyan Chapel in Bowerchalke where the service was conducted by Mary Ellen's uncle, the Rev. Richard Harding.

Frederick and Mary Ellen had three children; Muriel Yeoman, Frederick Henry and their youngest child, Herbert Butler – The Half-Shilling Curate.

But who was The Half-Shilling Curate? I searched high and low but after 100 years, I have found the man – a philosopher, guide, leader of men and most of all, my grandfather …

Herbert grew up in a close-knit, warm, family homestead. His father, Frederick was not only a devout Wesleyan Methodist minister and a loving father, but also a great naturalist. He was enchanted by the animal kingdom from the collection and study of butterflies to the observations on the behaviour of animals during the changing seasons of the year. Herbert shared his father's fascination and passion for all aspects of nature and the countryside. Frederick and his children thrived on learning the Latin names for flowers and plants and when time and opportunity permitted, they often went out on long walking expeditions to discover new species of plants and to watch and study animals in their natural habitat.

Three Cowl children: Eric, Muriel & Herbert c.1895. (Author's collection)

Herbert spent his early years growing up in Harrogate with his elder siblings. At the age of five, he and the family moved to Bournemouth and whenever the Rev. F.B. Cowl was called to a new circuit,[1] the family would uproot and move to their new home. On the census return of 1891, the Rev. F.B. Cowl was detailed as a 'Wesleyan Parson' and the family had a 'lady help' and a servant to assist Mary Ellen with the family home and the upbringing of Herbert and his siblings. Mary Ellen cherished her husband very much and supported him in all that he did.

Little is known of Herbert's formative years and his formal education. Much of his early life was spent in Bournemouth and London but whenever they could the family headed towards the Isle of Purbeck and New Forest areas and this is where he first learned to enjoy, name and understand plants, animals and birds. It was in the New Forest that he first discovered one of his favourite birds, the skylark – a bird that was to mean so much more to him years later in the trenches of war-torn Belgium.

In 1893, the Cowl family moved to Highgate where they stayed for three years before returning to the Bournemouth circuit in 1896. In 1899, the family moved again and Frederick Cowl's new circuit was in Wandsworth, South London. Three years later, in 1902, they moved to Hertford in Hertfordshire and Herbert attended Hertford Grammar School. He enjoyed playing football for the school and often attended football matches against other schools in the area. A year later the Headmaster of Hertford Grammar

1   A geographical area divided into smaller groups of churches known collectively as a circuit.

Herbert – the snake catcher.
(Author's collection)

School chose Herbert to become the new Head Boy for the school.[2] He became the senior boy taking on responsibilities for the students and representing the school on official occasions. He would have also known the young schoolboy, W.E. Johns who would later become the writer and creator of ace pilot and adventurer 'Biggles'.

At this time in Herbert's life he had already engaged with many hobbies and interests, including the art of snake-hunting. In February 1904 the school magazine, *The Hertfordian*, published an article under the title, 'Personal Experiences of H.G.S. Boys'- 'A day's snake-hunting in the New Forest'. Although written anonymously, the writing is very reminiscent of that of Herbert's and describes a scene in the New Forest which he would have known so well – this article is believed to be the hand of Herbert Cowl. The photograph above, also suggests Herbert's ability to successfully hunt the snake:

> I passed on into the glorious forest, where the great trees seemed to vie with each other in stateliness and size, and where a sacred silence seems to reign supreme, broken only by the crack of a twig as some gay little squirrel leaps past from branch to branch. Then again the scene changes to tangled undergrowth, mixed with smaller trees. And here I approached with quiet, cautious footstep, for here,

2   Hertford Grammar School became Richard Hale School where an original wall plaque bears the names of all Head Boys throughout the school's history.

where a patch of the morning sun is seen, the snake may be found basking. Noiselessly I searched each bush, till at length my troubles were rewarded, as I saw, curled round in a pile of dead leaves, a beautiful brown and black body. Slowly the head rises and those piercing little eyes flashed for a moment only, and noiselessly that coil becomes a straight line …

In July 1905, Herbert's sister, Muriel (fondly known by the family as 'Mukie') married a farmer, James Trehane. Her new home was at the Trehane family farm in the village of Hampreston, Dorset. Mukie and James had four sons in the years between 1906 and 1913 but on the outbreak of war, Mukie volunteered and became a serving nurse with the British Red Cross.

After initially training to become a Methodist minister at theological college, their brother, Frederick Henry (affectionately known as 'Eric'), became a headmaster for the Cape Government in South Africa, but on his return to England at the beginning of 1915, he died unexpectedly after a short illness. His passing was so sudden, untimely, painful and such a shock to the family that they never spoke of his name again.

Herbert had grown up in a Wesleyan home and it would have been under his father's watchful eye that he developed his own interest and love for God and the church. It is not known exactly why and at what time in his life Herbert decided to become a Wesleyan minister and follow in his father's footsteps, although once Herbert wrote of his childhood:

The Cowl Family – Top left, Eric; centre, Muriel; right, Herbert; sitting, the Rev. F.B. Cowl & Mary Ellen c. 1900. (Author's collection)

My life began to take its shape in later school days: one thread was woven with its pattern quite deliberately by my parents … So far as religion was concerned; we took that as an essential of living. For them, it was the air they breathed, and by it their lives were ordered.

However, another turning point may have been when he attended the famous London Crusade at the Royal Albert Hall in February 1905. His parents were then living in Hertfordshire, but Herbert stayed in Wandsworth whilst he visited the prestigious Royal Albert Hall in South Kensington. For two months at the beginning of the year, the well-known American evangelist and educator, Reuben Archer Torrey, was preaching there with his former student, Charles M. Alexander and it was reported that tens of thousands of professed conversions took place during this religious crusade. Herbert wrote to his mother with great excitement:

… at about 3 o'clock Mr Alexander mounted the dais shouting out "Light!! What we want is light, more light!! Tell those stewards to turn on the light!" then announcing that we would sing 'The Light of the World is Jesus.' His conducting is wonderful. He seems to draw the music out of the whole audience and mould it in his hands just as he likes. He picks up the voice of that great choir in his hand and throws it out over the congregation! So vast is the Hall however, that were he to stop his swinging, swaying body and arms, for one note, the whole congregation would immediately go altogether wrong, but for his motions it is impossible to tell the time of the singing. After some time Dr Torrey rises and calls in a loud, reverent voice, "Let us draw near to God in prayer" and one of the attendant ministers leads in prayer. Then the announcements and collection. More hymns, and then Dr Torrey, reverent, slow and firm, mounts the dais. Again "Let us draw near in to God in Prayer! Let us all stand as we Pray!" And a great hush falls upon that vast concourse. Then follows a prayer, simple, deep, straight to the point, mighty; the whole tone and atmosphere of which is summed up in the first great word, which echoes through the Hall and seems to stretch up in child-like expectation right into Heaven – "F-a-t-h-e-r!" No man who knows anything of the great prayer-life, can but sit down at the close of that prayer with a new thrill of hope and a deeper faith in this great power.

Herbert concludes his description of Dr Torrey to his mother:

He has no attraction of personality or style, I believe, yet he has entirely won me, because he is such a man of prayer.

At the age of 19 in 1905, Herbert was studying theology as a student in preparation for life as a Wesleyan Methodist minister and boarding at Cliff College, Hope Valley in Calver, Derbyshire which was a preliminary college for the ministry. Cliff College, a Georgian house and chapel set in landscaped grounds next to the River Derwent provided Evangelical training for the Wesleyan students. The close proximity of the River Derwent also provided fine waters for Herbert to pursue his interest in the art of fly-fishing. When he left Cliff College in 1906, the school register noted that he was 'Accepted for the Home Ministry'.

However, Herbert's official date of entrance into the Wesleyan Theological College at Headingley, was in September 1907 when he joined approximately fifty to sixty other students in residence who were between the ages of twenty and twenty five and wishing to enter the ministry. His studies included Methodist History, Polity, Homiletics, Pastoral Teaching of the Gospels, English Literature of the eighteenth century, Greek and Latin, as well as the Old and New Testaments. In the summer of 1908 he wrote home to his mother advising her of the progress with his studies:

> First Exam over this morning – Greek. Fair Time. Next on Wed. of next week. Preaching at Stanley this week-end, very small place, described as 'poor', but we will do our best.

By 1909 Herbert was beginning to prepare for his final examinations. At the beginning of his final academic year at Headingley College in November, one of Herbert's fellow students wrote in The Methodist Times:

> The routine of college life has settled down upon us all – to the new men the experience is too strange to be irksome – to the older students it is unconsciously loved or else consciously hated, according as they have or have not the scholastic temperament.

Headingley College, Leeds. (Author's collection)

Herbert in his Headingley College study, known as 'The Den' c.1909.
(Author's collection)

Life would not have been easy at Headingley. The college, a large impressive stone building (which opened in 1868), housed a central tower with a clock and ornate dome. There were multiple elaborate windows with wide stone steps running up to the front door which was flanked by lawns. However, the college gave the appearance, to some, of being much like a workhouse – cold long bare corridors, polished concrete flooring, silence reigning throughout and all matters being managed by the Governor and the Matron. A full day of strict study was brought to a close at the end of the day by the sound of the gong for prayers and supper in the hall with all the college students and staff.

Despite the disciplined regime of study, the students, on the whole, enjoyed their time at Headingley College. As well as Herbert's theological studies he was able to enjoy his love of poetry. In his later life Herbert met and became a good friend to Walter de la Mare and a great admirer of the poet, Edward Thomas. Herbert also enjoyed the games and sport offered at the college which included tennis and football.

As part of his studies during this time, Herbert continued (by invitation) to practise his new vocation preaching as a local preacher in the local communities in and around Yorkshire. One of the areas selected was Howden in the East Riding and one Sunday whilst preaching, Herbert saw the girl who was to become his future 'sweetheart', Mary Louise Townsley. Mary, known as May, was the only daughter of a Yorkshire landowner, William Townsley and his wife, Lilly Jane, a Canadian pioneer's daughter who lived at Foggathorpe House in Foggathorpe. William Townsley was a steward at Foggathorpe Chapel (a prestigious position within the community) and it was due to this position in the church and following general protocol that Mr Townsley invited the young Wesleyan student to have 'tea' with his family at his home following the Sunday service.

At the beginning of 1909, Herbert wrote home to his parents from Headingley College. Most of these letters talked of life in the college, tuck boxes and treats from home, services, missionary work and preaching schedules. Sometimes, he signed his letters home, 'The Half-Penny Curate' – as opposed to 'The Half-Shilling Curate' used in later years. However, he began to write about another matter which was praying on his mind:

> And now, since you insist on knowing what I meant by saying I was 'off colour', I suppose I must confess! I thought you would put two and two together, and conclude. I did not tell you, because I did not want to worry either of you with it. Now that I am more or less composed, you may as well know. This is, I need hardly say, very strictly private.
>
> The fact is that the girl I mentioned to you, at Foggathorpe, I have felt, as you say, to be the girl: seeming to possess all the qualities which my ideal specifies. (You will say, what I say myself, "Having seen so little of her?" and yet I seem driven to say – "yes".)

Foggathorpe Wesleyan Chapel, East Riding of Yorkshire.
The first time Herbert set eyes on the young Mary Louise Townsley. (John Leake)

Herbert knew that she was the girl for him – it was genuine love at first sight. However as an un-ordained Methodist minister, he would have realised that he was unable to pursue his great feelings for her for another five years. He would have to be fully ordained in 1914 before he was able to consider offering May marriage and a secure future. In his next letter home a few days later, following a letter from his parents, he writes to his mother:

> I must confess to finding it much harder than I had expected to forget: but I am doing my best, and the matter is by now almost banished to the realm of the subconscious.

A few days later, Herbert learnt that the whole Townsley family, May, her two younger brothers and her parents, had decided to relocate and return permanently to British Columbia. He writes back to his concerned parents:

> Don't worry: I have shelved the whole matter: – but it's a precious hard wrench. Don't suppose I shall see her again – and better not.

A week later, Herbert's inward torment is shown in the following extract from a letter to his father:

> For some time I put the whole matter by, tried to persuade myself that it was all foolishness: tried to forget it all in work, jollity, and devotion. Then it all welled up and took possession of my mind again; and I could not cast it off. This afternoon I met her in the City – partly by accident, though I suspected she would be there: she comes in every Thursday. We only spoke casually, for a few minutes, of course. I need not describe the effect upon myself, save to say that it has beaten into brain and heart what is there already, more deeply.

In the same letter, he addresses his mother's concerns:

> Please tell Mother, in reply to her letter, that I don't suppose she or her people have even a suspicion of it: I have tried to prevent it. I know that it will come out right in the end, and that God will order my way; but I have to do it. I think a quiet weekend, with some real worship and prayer will help to balance things up. Pray, won't you, little people? That kind of moral bias, and spiritual influence, which comes from other's prayers, means so much to a man at a time when it's hard to make up one's mind, doesn't it?

The Townsleys were preparing for their move to Canada and Herbert was beginning to study for his final exams at college. He described his room, also known to him as 'The Den':

I have just got a very nice frame for the photo of Mukie and her 'little flock'! She does look so sweet, perched on my wall beside my 'swot table'. You repose next to her, like a kind of guardian angel (to her, and to me!) Father still surmounts you both in his ecclesiastical chair: still smiles his dear old smile: and fans the flickering flame of swat 'when vagrant wishes beckon me astray'!

At some point a picture of Mary Louise Townsley was added to his collection of family photographs. In a subsequent letter, Herbert wrote of his next steps regarding his dilemma concerning his feelings for May:

I am preaching at Howden, 6 miles from Foggathorpe. Shall walk over, or train to Selby and thence to Foggathorpe, on Monday morning. I wrote Mrs Townsley and asked her if it would be quite convenient for me to come sometime during the day. She wrote me such a nice letter in reply, asking me most heartily to as early in the morning as possible, and stay the day. But her letter contained bad news indeed: they go in a month, or 6 weeks at the latest! Time was the thing for which I had most hoped, and upon which much depended. The most then that I can hope is that I can see sufficient of May before they go, to ask her Father's permission to write to her.

It seems May's father, William Townsley, was reluctant to give such endorsement at first as he and his wife had been hoping perhaps for a better and more appropriate class match for their daughter. However, the permission was granted and Herbert and May were able to continue their friendship with letters to and from British Columbia and England.

It was no secret to either family that Herbert and May adored each other, but in line with Wesleyan Church rules, until Herbert was ordained as a Methodist minister, he knew that he was in no position to marry her. He would have to wait. He only told a few of his closest friends at Headingley College about his feelings for May.

One day in early spring, just before the Townsley family were about to leave England, Herbert describes his after-dinner walk with May at Foggathorpe, the memory of which would last with him for the rest of his life and carry him through a world war.

For a little way Mrs Townsley walked with us till she seemed to have made us perfectly happy and at ease: then she left us. I wish you could have been there during that walk (at a respectable distance of course!). The land was bathed in the quiet spring sunlight. The larks had just begun their sweetest singing and all about the fields the lapwings swooping with their plaintive cries. And beside me was the sweetest dearest thing that all the spring could boast.

Herbert's exams were over and then it was Easter. He describes his last weekend seeing May before her travels:

Just back from Foggathorpe. Have had a wonderful weekend. Great times preaching, morning, afternoon and night. And a glorious long moonlight walk with May afterwards. I never before saw quite so much in her: she was just past all description!

Mr and Mrs Townsley, their daughter May (aged 17) and her two younger brothers left their Yorkshire home bound for a new life in Canada. They travelled in a second class cabin from Liverpool to Halifax, Nova Scotia on the ship 'Victorian', arriving in Canada on 27 April 1909. Their travel documents described them as 'Returning Canadians'.

Herbert continued his studies at Headingley College in Leeds. In Bristol on 16 March 1910 the Quarterly Meeting of the Clifton Circuit took place and the presiding superintendent,[3] the Rev. Richard B. Shepherd, reported to the meeting that they were looking to recruit a new minister for one of their churches and to replace the Rev. Ebenezer J. Ives.[4] The minutes of the meeting[5] detailed:

He [Rev. Shepherd] had consulted with the Chairman of the District and the stewards as to the probationer for Grenville [Chapel] and that they had asked that Mr Cowl, a son of Rev. F.B. Cowl and now at Headingley College be reserved for us [Clifton Circuit] at a salary of £100 p.a. [per annum].

The college results arrived – Herbert had passed his exams! At the meeting of the College's Discipline Committee held on 16 June 1910,[6] the Governor recorded that Herbert Butler Cowl was a 'diligent student, an earnest preacher' with 'reliable character'. By separate vote, Herbert was unanimously recommended for circuit work.[7]

Herbert missed May terribly. It was not long before he decided that he had to see her and the only way to do this would be for him to visit the Townsley family in British Columbia. He did not have the funds for such a journey but he knew that he had to find a way of getting to Canada.

Herbert asked his father for a loan to pay for the trip to May's family home in British Columbia. The cost of the voyage was calculated, noted in a small book (for father and son to record a schedule of repayments) and Herbert was able to raise enough money for his passage to North America. His intentions were honourable and both families knew and understood this.

Two days after his college's Discipline Committee Meeting, on 18 June 1910, Herbert, clergyman, aged 23, arrived at Lime Street Railway Station in Liverpool

---

3   Senior minister of the circuit.
4   *Western Daily Press*, 1 September 1910.
5   Bristol Records Office: Clifton Circuit, Bristol Quarterly Meeting Minutes.
6   Methodist Archives and Research Centre (MARC), Wesleyan Theological Institution, Headingley Branch, Minutes of Board of Discipline.
7   Bristol Records Office: NRA 17791 Clifton Circuit, Accs 32397, 37979.

where he hailed a cab to the port. After purchasing his ticket the next step was a cup of tea so he found 'a rather greasy little tea room on the quay', where he watched passengers boarding the great '*Lusitania*'. She sailed at 5:00 p.m. and S.S. *Dominion* took her place on the quayside.

Herbert boarded the White Star Liner S.S. *Dominion* ready to set sail for Montreal, Canada with 630 other passengers.

At 9.30pm, Herbert wrote to his 'Dearest little Mother':

> Two hours ago we lost sight of England. A mist, too lazy to be heavy, soon hid the low, unattractive coast. Bugle sounded for Dinner; tears are forgotten in gossip over the table. We are a strange table. Opposite me a row of real jolly Cornishmen, broad as they make them. Next to me a youth of about 17, off to a farm in Winnipeg, very young, and rather bumptious. Then a South African farmer (of whom more later). Then a Cornish U.M.C. [United Methodist Church] Minister. At other tables, there are all sorts: a Yankee, a German, a Scandinavian, etc. Some very attractive: some very – well, one would rather use a stick to touch them.

Herbert was fortunate because his cabin was upgraded from a small one with four berths to one twice the size with only one other sharing.

> After some time I found my companion: a tall sunburnt, honest-faced fellow. He informed me that there were several <u>Parsons</u> on board! So, I had to confess to being one myself. "What Church?" "Wesleyan" "Oh, that's my Church! See here." And he handed me a letter from a S. African Wesleyan Minister, saying that he (the bearer) was of a very old and well-known Methodist family, etc. I fairly jumped round the cabin! Then I picked up the "Cornish Parson", so have 3 or 4 chums when the voyage is 3 or 4 hours old! Tonight the sea is unrippled, and we are slipping along gloriously – to the West, and to the "gold"!

Herbert began to settle into a routine on-board the ship.

> Today has been spent mainly in falling in with the passengers, and falling out with the sea. The last-peep on deck last night showed a hazy horizon, and an oily sea from which the moon was flashing a silver pathway. This morning (7.45 on deck) the coast of Ireland (North) was just visible, the base of the coastland hills ruled in mist, their summit hid in cloud. Till we passed the extreme N.W. cape the sea was still as oil: since leaving there we have run into a little wind, and are now feeling a "ground swell". This has upset a number of the passengers. (I remain among the favoured well ones!)

Although he was excited by the adventure that lay ahead of him, he was not going to forget his faith:

Divine Service was held in the Saloon at 10.30 this morning, conducted by an American Parson: quite a nice fellow, with not too broad an accent, though hardly an English soul. Service consisted of simply Morning Prayer, introduced and concluded by a hymn. He gave no address of any kind. Some 70 folk attended. (I don't know what the 3rd Class passengers did in the way of service.)

As the days passed, Herbert began to experience the monotony of life on board.

I have come to the decision that it is very difficult to get to sleep on board. Beneath there is the hum and rattle of the engines, and with anything of a sea, the swish of scattered water. Above there is off and on the loud escape of steam, the crack of the marconigraph[8] (just like a hustled corncrake). Also till late at night the tramp of feet on the deck; and this again in the early morning – particularly when the men turn out to "sweep decks". Add to this a frequent violent hoot from the siren when the fog sets in thick – and you have an idea of some of the difficulties to be overcome.

The journey across the Atlantic was coming to an end.

This is our last day on the open seas. A strong North Eastern has sprung up, but it is too late to catch us: by tonight we shall be through the straits of Belle Isle. Just before lunch a hue and cry of "Iceberg!" was raised, and those of us who were keen–sighted enough made out on the misty horizon a huge, dim form of crystal. There was a biting wind and a stringing rain sweeping the deck, so that it was hard to see. It looked like a great shadowy ghost looming though the rain and driving spray; perhaps nearly twice as big as our own boat. But later a small block of ice, some 12 feet square above water, and of the most beautiful pale blue colour, passed within 20 yards of us. But it is so bitterly cold that one does best to keep below on a day like this: especially as it is pouring with rain that is almost like ice.

Herbert's love of nature, especially birds, was noted and his attention to detail was captured in his descriptive observations from the stern of the ship:

The sea birds are rather interesting, though not various. The commonest are some grey gulls which seem to follow the ship. They are the most skilful birds on the wing I have ever seen. They seem to wheel about with the tip of one wing about a millimetre off the water, yet skimming the steepest and most broken waves without ever wetting a feather. In the teeth of the storm I noticed two tiny

8   Apparatus used in Marconi wireless telegraphy.

Petrels, who seemed to have caught the spirit of the wind and wave, and were flitting and swooping madly over the breaking crests and down along the steep troughs of water.

The sea crossing concluded with magnificent sights of the great hills of Newfoundland, Quebec and finally Montreal.

The next stage of his adventure was to travel by train across Canada from East to West Coast. In a letter to his parents he wrote the following:

> The train journey was <u>magnificent</u>, each of the three distinct sections giving its own wonder: first, the long span of Scotch-like scenery: – small thickly growing trees, winding rivers and low hills: next the great span of prairie first cut into innumerable tiny farms; but later changing to one huge stretch of bleak, brown, undulating waste, miles and miles again, sun scorched and relentless, but magnificent in its very immensity. Last came the mountains: first the Rockies, then the finer cascades.

Herbert had hoped to have a sleeper across Canada but they had all been booked by the time he reached the ticket office. So, he had to travel without that luxury:

> This brought an average of about 2 hrs sleep a night, except Friday, when I got none! And yet I was fresh and well all the way!

When Herbert arrived in Vancouver, May's two brothers met him at the North Vancouver Ferry. The three young men crossed the water to North Vancouver where they caught an 'electric car (!)' [the tram] to the area where the Townsley's 'sweet little wooden house with a big veranda' was located amidst 'a medley of rich bracken, tall willow herb, and great blackened, gnarled tree stumps'. Herbert describes the moment that he arrived outside their house:

> On the veranda were standing Mrs Townsley and – just <u>exactly</u> the same Little Girl I said goodbye to! And yet not <u>just</u> the same: rather sweeter and more refined looking than ever. Both gave me a welcome worth all the journey.

At this point, Herbert had begun to use a new pet name for May – she had become his dear 'Maisie'. The letter continues:

> Mr Townsley was away in Vancouver Island: but he turned up very unexpectedly just before dinner. And though he alone persists in calling me "Mr Cowl", yet he is kindness itself to me: he even insists that I shall not have 5 cents expense while I am here! I am never allowed (when they know, that is!) even to pay my own train fares, much less Maisies!

Once settled in North Vancouver, Herbert wrote home again to his 'Dearest Little Mother'.

And what's a man to do now? Here I am on a beautiful veranda, where the only bit of cool is to be found: down at the foot of the hills stretches the sound as still as sleep, save for here and there a motor boat and the ferry plying to and fro. Behind the great mountains are towering, outlined black against the glowing 'embers of the day'. This alone is enough to make one stop everything and only think of wonder. But need I tell you that there is something far more wonderful here? Beside me in the hammock is lying the most beautiful girl – I will be very temperate, and say – in British Columbia. And when one knows her, and knows that that is only the expression of the inner life, Well, do you wonder that it has taken me from 3 to 6 to write a page?

During his stay in North Vancouver he spent as much time as he could with May, met her Canadian relatives and preached at their local churches in Sardis, Chilliwack and North Vancouver. Whilst visiting Chilliwack, Herbert met Mrs Townsley's parents, Canadian pioneers, affectionately known as A.C. Wells and Sarah Manetta, May's much loved grandparents.

Mr and Mrs Wells lived at Edenbank, Chiliwack and Herbert was taken by the Townsley family to meet May's grandparents. Herbert describes another memorable journey:

First a walk of a few hundred yards from the house to the tram, through thick, powdery dust, and over board paving. Then a 5 minutes tram running down the hill to the ferry (remember that every road is perfectly straight here, very wide, and runs always at right angles to every other that crosses it: Avenues up and down, streets across.) The larger ferry will carry several hundred people upstairs, with Ladies Room and Smoking Room downstairs and open deck for carts and horses. They run every half hour, and take 15 minutes to cross the inlet. Then we took a car to Mr Townsley's office, and while the ladies rested, he and I went out and bought fruit and cake for the train.

The train left at 4.30pm and dawdled up through the rich bush, red with willow herb or white with fox-gloves, wound along the shore of the inlet, or skirted the feet of ragged mountains or foothills, reaching Harrison Mills at 7.15pm. This, though as crow flies it is only 70 or 80 miles from Vancouver to Chilliwack! At Harrison Mills we waited on the little ferry for nearly an hour: but it was well worthwhile. Harrison Mills is a tiny settlement with a big timber mill, bunched up in a big cup of mountains, great lines and points of mountain closing in on every side save where the Harrison River winds through. It is along its banks that the Railway just finds a bare footing. I never saw water of such a colour – a deep, rich, emerald green: and right opposite us the steep hillside climbed from the water side covered with foliage of all kinds, a dozen shades of green and here and there a spray of Ivy Maple of a dark red colour. With a brilliant moon right up we steamed down the river for a mile or two, till sudden clouds of white mud came puffing into the green river water: this told that we were entering the Fraser River where the two unite. This is a wicked river: yellow brown in colour, gurgling with sudden hidden currents and whirlpools, and clogged with great snags (huge tree roots torn away in wild weather) It is a very dangerous river, even the Indians are afraid of it.

In the settling twilight we forced our way through the sweeping current to the river bank, 5 or 6 miles from Harrison Mills. Here Ernest [May's youngest brother] was waiting with a Democrat (a buggy with double seat, one behind the other) and we jolted and jumped through the clouds of dust, and quiet moonlight to Edenbank. (Mrs Townsley and Ernest in front; Maisie and I behind, with a big pail of cherries between us!) Chilliwack is about 3 miles from the landing, Edenbank 2 miles from Chilliwack.

The house is situated in a wide valley, surrounded almost completely with mountains. The valley, once thick bush and forest, is now tamed down to quiet pastures, hay fields, and hop plantations, and has a population of 2 or 3 thousand.

Herbert describes May's very dear grandparents to his parents:

Mr Wells is a very fine old man, now very bent and worn. But he has been very tall and strong. He impresses you immediately as being of sterling character and unflinching principle. He has little to say, but what he says is right to the point. Mrs Wells is a dear old lady, short and white haired, with a strong, beautiful, troubled face: she can hardly see at all now. Happily, for at least my peace of mind, Mr Wells took a great liking to me, they say.

Whilst at Chilliwack staying with Mr and Mrs Wells, Herbert was asked to preach in their local churches.

On Sunday, May, the housekeeper, and I drove in to Chilliwack for morning service, where I preached. The church is square and small, seating about 300: about half full. They were difficult folk to get hold of, on the whole: I had a very difficult time, and did not do much, I fear. But after a lovely afternoon in a hay field with the Little Girl, was in better form for the evening. I was preaching at Sardis (Carman Church), about a mile up the road from Edenbank, on the edge of the forest at the foot of a mountain. The little church was full. Mr and Mrs Wells were there: Mrs Townsley and the boys; Mrs Townsley's brother and his wife; and of course Maisie. Things went well: I had a great time. It was comparatively cool – not over 90 degrees in the shade, as it was the two following days! So everything went splendidly: and the folk seemed hugely elated.

British Columbia, June 1910 – May (also affectionately known as Maisie) and Herbert relaxing together under Capilano Bridge, North Vancouver. (Author's collection)

Over the following weeks Herbert and May continued to enjoy their time together. May showed Herbert the local neighbourhood, some of the beauty spots and introduced him to the Indian village of Squamish. The letters home continued and Herbert described some of their special time together and joked with his parents illustrating his sense of humour too:

> Well, here comes the Victoria boat through the narrows, and that reminds me it is nearly time to be off with the Little Girl over the water: first to the office to tease Mr Townsley, and ask him to come to the shore with us and paddle; then on to the beach at Kitisilano and then the Band Concert at English Bay and home by about 9.30.

It was on this trip that Herbert gave May a sapphire ring, a token of his feelings towards her and a ring to show his intention of marrying her one day. He even wrote to his parents with the news and including a description and a detailed illustration of the ring so that they would approve:

> You will be interested to know that this morning the Little Lady of the West is wearing my ring for the first time. It is a beautiful little 3 sapphire ring (blue, to

match her eyes – though there is a shade of grey in them, they are too uncommon to be blue). Something like that! She is so pleased with it. I went off to the city [Vancouver] this morning directly after breakfast and chose it.

It has all happened in this way: I found that Mr Townsley was very pleased at the idea of my coming out here like this: it has quite tickled his fancy, I believe!

May was anxious that I should say nothing for weeks, lest we should raise breezes. But I pointed out to her that I thought he would appreciate it more if I went straight to the point quite fearlessly. This turned out to be just right. I asked him when he could give me half an hour, and went over to his office with him yesterday morning. When we got to business I nearly toppled out of the office window 5 stories down; for he was just as nice and kind as could be.

Herbert was delighted that Mr Townsley had accepted that his intentions were serious and sincere. He concludes:

Oh, I did want to scatter all the Insurance Policies in the office out over the City with mighty shouts of glory!

In Herbert's last letter home in the middle of July he writes of the pressure and strain on May:

Of all our doings I must tell you later. Need I say that we two have already had some never-to-be-forgotten times? Sometimes I fear a little, the strain of it all on her. She feels deeply and silently: the more deeply the more silent and the long strain on waiting, the eagerness of the last few weeks, and now the relief, etc., is rather a heavy strain on her, I fear.

However, Herbert and May would have to wait until Herbert was an in a position to offer her a secure future as the wife of a Wesleyan minister. With their deep abiding love for each other, they knew that somehow, one day they would be together.

The Canadian adventure was over and Herbert left British Columbia for Quebec. The twenty three year old clergyman returned to Montreal and set sail for England aboard the Canadian Northern Line's Royal Edward, second class and bound for Bristol.[9] Herbert arrived back in England on 25 August 1910.

In the late summer of 1910 Herbert moved to Bristol and was living in a two-bedroom residence at 32 Caledonia Place, Clifton where he was to begin his life as a Wesleyan minister at Grenville Chapel, sometimes referred to as Grenville Place Chapel, Oldfield Place, in Hotwells on the Clifton Circuit. One of the local

9   The National Archives (hereafter TNA): United Kingdom Incoming Passenger Lists.

newspapers, the *Western Daily Press*, described the young probationer in his first year as, 'being a young man with much promise'.[10]

Herbert's first formal meeting in Bristol at his new circuit was on 9 September 1910 when he attended the Church Leader's Meeting. From this first meeting onwards Herbert was plunged into the busy life of his new Ministry. In the minutes his new responsibilities were recorded including; church meetings, harvest festival, musical services and various other public meetings. His long training was now being put into action.

On 21 September 1910, Herbert attended his first official Quarterly Meeting of the Clifton Circuit held at Victoria Wesleyan Church. He was welcomed into the Circuit and along with several other new recruits, he was told by the presiding minister, the Rev. B. Bean, 'hopefully that the work of God may prosper in the Circuit during their Ministry'. Herbert was paid £25 quarterly with additional expenses as and when required paid separately.

Herbert was detailed as being 'On Trial' [on probation] for those first few years as a minister in the Bristol and Bath District.[11] He continued his studies and learnt the finer points of becoming a Methodist minister. At the end of his first year, the Superintendent's Report (in the Bristol and Bath District Minute Book) detailed:

> His pulpit ministrations, diligent pastoral attention have won for him the esteem and love of the whole circuit.

Although Herbert's work and responsibilities were spread throughout the Circuit, his main commitment was to Grenville Chapel (occasionally referred to as Grenville Church).

By the end of the second year his work was described as being 'eminently satisfactory'. At this time he had formed a Junior Society Class for the boys, a weekly girls' club which soon became extended to three meetings a week, a young men's club and a football club for the boys at Grenville Chapel. He was also involved with the opening of the new premises of the Y.M.C.A. in Hotwells.[12] Herbert was beginning to make his mark and thriving in the work of his community. At the last Quarterly Meeting of the Clifton Circuit held at Portland Chapel, Kingsdown, Bristol in 1912, it was detailed:

> Mr Hobley reported that subject to Conference, Rev. H.B. Cowl had accepted an invitation to remain in the circuit a fourth year. The news was received with acclamation.

---

10   *Western Daily Press*, 1 September 1910.
11   Wesleyan Methodist Conference Agendas 1910-13.
12   *Western Daily Press*, 23 May 1911.

In 1913 the annual Wesleyan Methodist Conference minutes[13] showed that 'Herbert B. Cowl' was 'under the direction and tutelage of the Rev. Samuel Body'. Although deeply engrossed in his new role at Grenville Chapel, Herbert found himself thinking of May more and more. They continued to write long letters to each other and Herbert sent postcards of Clifton and his new surroundings to British Columbia. On one occasion he wrote to May on the back of a picture postcard showing a scene of The Downs in Clifton:

> This is a bit of "my Temple", as I call it – the Observatory hill, which I must often have mentioned to you. The river runs, and the ships pass, between the Giant's Head and the woods opposite. It is in those woods that the nightingale sings. I spend many a midnight hour up here.

The summer of 1913 was long, sunny and golden, with no sign of the storm clouds that would arrive in 1914. This was the last year of the Victorian age.

Herbert's studies were on-going and every year whilst on probation he was assessed and examined in four key areas; Greek, Hebrew, essay (on a given theme) and Wesley (teachings of the New Testament and selected sermons). Not all ministers had to speak, read and write Hebrew, but like many men from an earlier generation, Herbert continued with the subject despite only achieving 44% in his last exam. However, the final judgement of the committee in May 1914 read; 'moderate exam results but excellent circuit reports'. At the same time, the Superintendent's Report (in the Bristol and Bath District Minute Book)[14] concluded:

> Herbert B Cowl: Very high character and great pastoral fidelity. Gives himself to his work with almost too little restraint.

It was not until later in 1914 that he was formally recorded as being, 'admitted into Full Connexion with the Conference'. In total Herbert spent the best part of four years at Grenville Chapel where he learnt the practical skills of working as a Wesleyan minister and also won the admiration of the young men (and women) in his congregation, especially as he pursued his interest in football as the Chairman and President of the Grenville Wesleyan Amateur Football Club.[15]

On 17 June 1914, Herbert attended his last Quarterly Meeting of the Clifton Circuit held at Victoria Church in Bristol. At the meeting, it was proposed:

> That the thanks of the meeting be given to Rev. H.B. Cowl for his Ministry in the Circuit for the past four years, this resolution was passed unanimously and

---

13   A volume published at the time of the annual Wesleyan church gatherings.
14   MARC, Bristol and Bath District Minute Book 1912-14.
15   *Western Daily Press*, 28 March 1914.

Herbert the keen fisherman; location and date unknown. (Author's collection)

with acclamation, many members speaking with great feelings as to Mr Cowl's work in all parts of the Circuit and his Ministry to the young people and children being especially mentioned.

Before the annual Wesleyan Methodist Conference at Leeds, a meeting at Woodhouse Moor Church took place to examine the candidates for ordination. The young men were questioned on their judgement, their suitability as men fit for their work and their testimony in terms of their conversion and their call to their new challenges as Methodist ministers. Herbert spoke of the home influences and also commented:

All the joy that had come to him at conversion he could never explain. His strength as a minister was in his confidence in Christ, and if Christ were taken out of life, then his call to preach would be gone.

It was a proud moment for father and son. The day before the conference, the Rev. F.B. Cowl was voted onto the Legal Hundred – a prestigious position, being chosen to be one of the top hundred most recognised senior Wesleyan ministers in the church.

After nearly four years in the Clifton Circuit, at 10:00 a.m. on Tuesday 28 July 1914, Herbert was formally ordained into the Methodist church at The Leeds Conference in Brunswick Church.[16] His father was one of several ministers who assisted the President, ex-President and Secretary of the Conference during the Ordination Service where the ex-President gave a long address which included the topics; the call to preach, dangers in the path, social temptations, self-discipline and soul culture.

Little did Herbert and his father know that this day was also the day when Austro-Hungary declared war on Serbia and as a consequence the world was heading towards calamity. Herbert moved to Street in Somerset and his life as a fully-fledged Wesleyan Methodist minister began in the Mid-Somerset Mission. He was 28 years old.

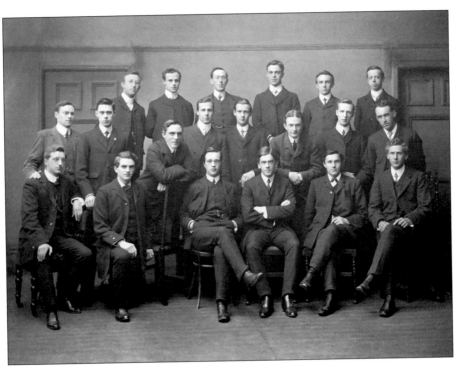

Herbert, middle left (leaning on the back of a chair) with some of his fellow students at Headingley College.

16   *The Methodist Recorder* and *The Methodist Times* and Author's Private Papers, August 1914.

2

The Outbreak of War

On 4 August 1914, the British Government declared a state of war with Imperial Germany. The Wesleyan Church along with the other churches responded swiftly to the call of duty. The Emergency Committee of the Wesleyan Army and Navy Board met two days later to further discuss the War Office's request for chaplains to be appointed in the home camps and for overseas active service.

As the summer months of 1914 passed, the war in Europe spread to the far corners of the world. Young men were recruited from all classes of society across the British Empire. On behalf of the mother country, civilian volunteers would don uniforms for King and Country. For its part, Secretary for State for War, Lord Kitchener called for the raising of the New Armies as a substantial reinforcement to the already deployed British Expeditionary Force (BEF).

The civilian population of the British Isles rallied to support the war effort. The close links between the nonconformists and the Liberal Party also helped to underpin the co-ordinated approach with support for the military on the home front. The Rev. Dinsdale Young (President of the Wesleyan Conference and ex-pupil of Headingley College) described the armed forces as fighting for 'a righteous cause' and proposed the wish for a 'patriotism which sought the spiritual good of the nation'.[1] Faith and patriotism were inextricably linked at the beginning of the war. Faith was treated as as moral compass for all.

The Wesleyan Church was anxious to give its full support to the war effort and thus to demonstrate the importance of Wesleyan patriotism! The nonconformists were encouraged to send support to the National Relief Fund which had been set up by the Prince of Wales. Many young men rushed to volunteer in the belief that the war would be over before Christmas.

On 9 September 1914, Herbert hosted the Mid Somerset Mission thirty seventh Quarterly Meeting at the Wesleyan church in Street, Somerset. The minutes recorded: 'The meeting cordially endorsed the welcome of the Mission Stewards, to the Rev. H.B. Cowl newly appointed Minister at Street.'

---

1   *The Methodist Times*, 24 December 1914.

The country was facing much change, as was the church, with an alarming decline in service attendance of all denominations before the war. Society was changing too. In an article published in *The Methodist Recorder* at the end of 1914, Herbert's father, the Rev. F.B. Cowl, described as an 'honoured minister', was interviewed asking his opinion on changes in society regarding 'Life's Impetuous Tide':

> Many earnest people, seeking an explanation of the declining religious life of this country prior to the War, found it – in part, at least – in the decay of parental authority in the home.

Despite the decrease in the active numbers of worshippers, Christianity still under-pinned society. The Christian principals of fairness and justice were part of a proud British heritage and baptisms, marriages and burials formed the cornerstones of Christianity. Nevertheless, there were some people within the church who had strong beliefs and thought that with regard to war, fighting was immoral. However, nearly a month after the bloody Battle of Mons (where the British Expeditionary Force was forced to commence an epic retreat), on Saturday 19 September 1914, the *Western Daily Press* published an article concerning the Wesleyan District Synod[2] in the Bristol and Bath District and its views on the changing situation in Europe.

> This Synod regards with horror the devastating war now raging throughout Europe. It is, however, absolutely convinced that the British Government acted the part of peacemaker and did not relax its efforts until all hope of success had finally disappeared, and that our country only drew the sword when plighted faith and national safety left no alternative course.
>
> Britain's part, therefore, in the war is one on which she can appeal for victory to the God of righteousness and peace, and one which she must prosecute until success crowns her efforts. The crisis through which we are passing is one of unparalleled magnitude and solemnity. The liberties, not of Britain only, but of Europe, would perish if German militarism should conquer.
>
> The Synod recognises with satisfaction and pride the alacrity with which the young manhood of our Church has responded, and is responding, to the call of their country, in its hour of need, and has every confidence that our people will continue to do their duty at this grave crisis in our history.
>
> This Synod rejoices in the fact that the Wesleyan Methodist Church is devoting itself to the work of relieving the wounded, comforting the bereaved, providing for the needs of refugees, and assisting in every possible way in the administration of all funds that are seeking to relieve distress; and it is confident that our people will continue to give all the practical assistance that is possible.[3]

2   Annual or biannual meeting of ministers or lay circuit representatives within the District.
3   *The Western Daily Press*, 14 September 1914.

In November, the leaders of the Mid Somerset Mission[4] held a circuit meeting where discussions took place regarding various matters concerning the church in the local area. The following was discussed and minuted (although Herbert was not present at this meeting):

> With regards to the Castle Cary appointment, the name of the Rev. H.B. Cowl of Street was suggested. It was resolved that the Rev. H.B. Cowl of Street, be invited to become second Minister stationed at Castle Cary in 1915 with the suggestion that his decision might be deferred until after Christmas.

This would indicate that at the time of the meeting on 4 November 1914, the Mid Somerset Mission were not aware of Herbert's possible intentions of becoming an Army Chaplain. There was also a quarterly list of public services and he was scheduled to preach at various locations in the area during January, so during the following month it would have come as a surprise to learn that they would lose their minister to the war effort.

On 16th December the German High Seas Fleet attacked four seaport towns in the north-east of England with the intention of damaging British morale. The result was 137 fatalities and 592 wounded. This could well have been the last in a series of events that finally made Herbert feel that it was now time to volunteer and become a British Army Chaplain.

Herbert could have easily kept himself out of the war or even returned to Canada. Compulsory military service, conscription, was not introduced until 1916 but men in Holy Orders or regular Ministers of any denomination were exempt. However, he felt without doubt that it was his duty and with a strong desire to help in the war effort he waited for news from the church.

The hierarchy of the Wesleyan church and the Wesleyan Army and Navy Board considered his suitability to join the BEF. Earlier in the year Herbert would have ordinarily followed a similar path to that which his father had taken in the church, concentrating on pastoral ministry in churches and schools. With no military background in his family, it would have been an unlikely thought that he would have considered becoming an Army Chaplain or of travelling to a front line or a battle zone. However, as the country faced its darkest hour, Herbert knew that this was what he wanted to do.

The final copy of *The Methodist Times* in 1914 reflected on the mood of the country and gave the following report to its younger readers, looking at the past twelve months and looking forward to peace in the New Year:

> Poor Old Year! Poor 1914! It has witnessed terrible things. It has seen truth and honour trampled on. It has seen sorrow, suffering, and death.

---

4   Bristol Records Office, NRA 17791 Clifton Circuit, Accs. 32397, 37979.

Among it all, boys and girls of the British Empire should remember that the war was forced upon us; that we are fighting for our national life, for the honourable keeping of promises and treaties, without which there could be no peace, no order, no advancement, and indeed, no civilisation.

Remember this, all of you – we all must remember it – and it will help us to bear any trouble or pain that may come to us.

We hope and we pray that the New Year may bring peace once more, and – of this I am sure – the braver, the stronger we are, the sooner peace will come. We all have to help, the men and the women, the boys and the girls. I am sure that 1915 will bring something that everyone can do. We all must be ready and willing to do that something when the time comes.[5]

The army, having reviewed Herbert's application, would have determined whether or not he had the desired qualities – the highest level of morale, discipline, offensive spirit and clerical expertise for the vacancy. Would he be able to address large bodies of men and equally would he be able to talk to an individual soldier? Herbert's ability to ride a horse and to speak a limited amount of French would have certainly helped him in terms of his suitability for active service. In addition, the Methodist circuit in Street, Somerset would have needed to provide ministerial cover for the local area so that their minister could be released from his duties, to join the armed forces.

General Sir Douglas Haig remarked during the early stages of the war:

We must have large minded, sympathetic men as parsons, who realise the Great Cause for which we are fighting, and can imbue their hearers with enthusiasm …[6]

He also recognised the value of the Army Chaplains in a separate statement in 1915, when he said; "A good chaplain is as valuable as a good general".

Herbert patiently waited for news from the War Office during the last weeks of December. Finally, following recommendation from the Wesleyan Board, he received a formal letter, posted to his new Hampshire address, from A.C. Strange, Secretary to the War Office (Alfred Charles Strange, a civil servant, Assistant Principal of the Chaplains Branch)[7] at the close of the month:

Sir, I am directed to inform you that you have been selected for temporary duty as an Acting Chaplain to the Forces, and should report yourself to the General Officer Commanding, Aldershot as early as possible, notifying to this office the date on which you join.

5   *The Methodist Times*, 24 December 1914.
6   Michael Snape, *The Royal Army Chaplains' Department, 1796-1953: Clergy Under Fire* (Woodbridge: Boydell Press, 2008), p. 219.
7   1914 War Office List.

The waiting was over. On Christmas Eve 1914, the young, newly-ordained Methodist minister, the Rev. Herbert Butler Cowl, signed up to the war effort and became a Temporary Chaplain to the Forces. The contract for a Temporary Chaplain to the Forces was for a 12 month period. (However Herbert, like so many of the Wesleyan Army Chaplains, would choose to continue his service to the church and the army for the duration of the war.)

On that same day, 24 December 1914, across the Channel, the celebrated 'Christmas Truce' was, among other places up and down the line, observed on the Ypres front. After nearly four months of bloodshed one of the bloodiest wars in history was taking its toll. For a brief moment, on Christmas Day, a seasonal exchange of traditional military courtesies and consequent expressions of peace and goodwill embraced both sides of 'no man's land'. Meanwhile, on Christmas Eve, one of Herbert's cousins, the Rev. Richard Winboult Harding, wrote in *The Methodist Times* regarding the necessity of faith in God and remembered Lincoln's answer to one who asked him if he thought God was on his side. Lincoln had simply replied, 'I hope I am on God's side'.

Having accepted a commission, on Christmas Day 1914, Herbert reported for duty at the Bordon Wesleyan Soldiers' Home near Aldershot in Hampshire to succeed the Rev. William Thomas Sharpley. Herbert, at 28 years of age, was a very young Army Chaplain, as most of them were well into their thirties, forties, fifties and even older! At this point in the war, there were only four Wesleyan Army Chaplains who were younger than Herbert,[8] and when he later began his service overseas, he was one of the very youngest to go to the front.

On Thursday 31 December 1914, the thirty eighth Quarterly Meeting of the Mid Somerset Mission, was held at the Wesleyan church in Castle Cary. The following was minuted:

> The Chairman informed the meeting that the Rev. H.B. Cowl of Street had been appointed as Chaplain to the Forces. The meeting expressed its regret at the loss of Mr Cowl's valued services, and desired a message of thanks to be sent to him, coupled with sincere wishes for his future success.

Army life would have brought many changes for Herbert. He had to adjust to his new way of life and face the challenges of his much changed uniform! His sombre black clerical cassock would be exchanged for a smart Khaki tunic – service dress cap, tunic, breeches and puttees. Some chaplains wore leather gaiters (often very highly polished), but Herbert preferred puttees. The art of wrapping them around his calves must have been a new perplexing experience. Instructions were provided; bind not too tight or too loose. Some black was retained in his new garments; buttons, badges and black belt. Overall the appearance of the uniform was of military smartness. For the first time as a commissioned officer with the rank of captain, Herbert had to become

8   Army List, Army Chaplains Department & Wesleyan Methodist Conference Minutes.

Sunday Parade Service, Bordon Camp. (Author's collection)

accustomed to being saluted. Initially the endless saluting may have been both tiring and very trying, but possibly a little gratifying with a faint glimmer of vanity! For some of the men it must have been a novelty to salute their parson too!

During this time, Herbert lived at 'Brantfell', a large detached house in Whitehill, a twenty minute walk from Bordon. The Wesleyan Soldiers' Home at Bordon comprised a chapel, a lecture hall (with seating for 300 men) and amongst other amenities, it had ten bedrooms, three baths and a suite for the residing chaplain. It was a single storey building constructed of wood with a dark green corrugated tin roof which overlooked the heather and pine trees covering the South Downs. A fenced garden surrounded the soldiers' home with landscaped flower beds and seating. It was a sanctuary where soldiers could find their Army Chaplain and a peaceful haven to rest and socialise. During Herbert's time there, a 'first class billiard table', as described in the Monthly Finance Meeting Minutes, was also purchased for the soldiers' entertainment and relaxation. At times, home camps did not have the best moral atmosphere; there were many distractions including drinking and gambling, so the provision of games rooms and other amenities in the Wesleyan Soldiers' Home contributed to a comfortable and healthy environment. At the North Camp Wesleyan Soldiers' Home Aldershot, there were even sports facilities including a large gymnasium as well as swimming baths! It was the Wesleyan church that had been instrumental in the introduction of Soldier's Homes and other similar institutions at army camps and nearby churches.

Herbert had been a strong supporter of the Temperance movement. Drunkenness in the ranks had been a great problem in the army and temperance and abstinence societies were created to combat the issue. These societies were usually founded by various church-based groups. At the beginning of the war, the Royal Army

Wesleyan Soldier's Home, Bordon Camp. (Author's collection)

Temperance Association had a membership of about 60,000 members. Many of these soldiers who resisted the lure of alcohol, the demon drink, received badges and medals in recognition for their professed abstinence. Herbert along with two of his cousins' husbands, who were also Army Chaplains, the Rev. Arthur Walters and the Rev. Arthur Stanley Bishop, with his new friend, the Rev. Sydney Jacoby were all involved with the Wesleyan Church's Temperance Committee.[9]

Some of Herbert's ministry included working with the soldiers at Longmoor Camp. There was a military railway which ran between the Bordon and Longmoor Military Camps – a distance of approximately four miles. The army's Woolmer Instructional Military Railway (WIMR – nicknamed 'Will It Move Railway'!) operated from Bordon Camp through the Woolmer Forest Firing Ranges to Longmoor Camp. Part of Herbert's new role was to identify Wesleyan army recruits entering the camps. Weekly lists were provided and it was his responsibility to 'hunt' them down in their billets. Given the size of the camps at Bordon and Longmoor, this would have been a very time consuming task. However, it would have been rewarding and an opportunity for Herbert to acquaint himself with the new arrivals.

Prior to the war in 1912, the Rev. J.H. Bateson had written an account[10] with regard to the value of the Wesleyan Soldiers' Homes in Aldershot:

> ... the influence of the Soldiers' Homes is helping to produce men of the right sort, and to prevent the moral deterioration of the fine type of young soldier now entering the Army in all parts of Great Britain.

9   MARC, Wesleyan Methodist Conference Minutes 1915.
10   Wesleyan Soldiers' Homes, Aldershot, Annual Report 1911-12.

In the early days of the war, there had been a certain amount of confusion regarding the religious denomination of servicemen. Also, denominational labels stood for old rivalries between the churches. There was a high percentage of soldiers inaccurately classified on their enrolment forms and some on-going confusion when they were given the opportunity of having their denomination detailed on their identification disc, also known as the 'dog tag'. The Wesleyan soldiers had 'W' or 'WES' engraved on their issue discs, along with their service number and name. Some soldiers had no strong objections to the label they were given whereas others were influenced by their companions and the recruiting sergeant. However, a religious affiliation dictated which Sunday Parade Service a soldier attended and in the event of death on active service, the information was utilised for burial purposes. In February 1915, the Rev. J.H. Bateston (Office of the Wesleyan Army and Navy Board in Westminster) wrote a letter re-enforcing the points of the 'Religious Rights of Wesleyan Soldiers' and to strengthen the case for, 'the right of every soldier wrongly attested to have the matter of his religious attestation corrected'.[11] Although, in many ways, the distinction between religious denominations counted for little, with many men, Wesleyan or not, the Army Chaplain was, in general, warmly received.

An Army chaplain's pay was ten shillings a day; allowances varied according to circumstance. Herbert commenced his military duties with the commissioned rank of captain. Nevertheless, most men would have simply address him as 'Padre'.

As a 'Temporary Chaplain to the Forces, 4th Class – Land Forces', he started his work with not all of his flock being Wesleyan Methodists. Herbert would have led some of the mandatory Parade Services in the camp, whilst giving the men 'spiritual fortitude and guidance' through their transformation, during this short training, from men to soldiers. These men would become his friends and comrades.

In December 1914, *The Methodist Recorder* published an article by Herbert's cousin, the Rev. R.W. Harding, in which he described and gave readers a taste of life as an Army Chaplain:

> Chaplaincy is not easy work. Yesterday I preached twice – we had 500 at morning parade, married the sergeant and his girl, took part in an open-air service, and in a great after-meeting, and helped with a tea for 450 soldiers.

The Rev. Harding also observed:

> One thing that impresses me more and more. In times of luxurious peace, we can discuss the decline of membership, theatre-going, Higher Criticism, and all sorts of other things. But at a crisis when Eternity is consciously only a step away, we are driven back instinctively on the Gospel of the glory of the Blessed God. Here are men under our hand who are face to face with Reality.

11   *My Wesleyan Methodist Ancestors*, Chaplains www.mywesleyanmethodists.org.uk

Next week, perhaps some of them may be lying cold and dead under the silent Belgian stars.

Herbert's work at Bordon was not altogether straightforward. Sunday was the one day in camp when a soldier was granted rest. Parade Service was compulsory and a large number of men resented their precious free time being taken up with the preaching of a Padre. Indeed, many bitterly resented the compulsory service attendance as they considered religion should be voluntary – this was a shock to Herbert:

> And those first days, from the bosom of a circuit to the raw of an army camp, were far from easy. To hear the flip of cards and the passing of money during the sermon of a Parade Service for men on their way to die was something of a shock. To be jeered and shouted down in a Service …

Despite Herbert's initial concerns regarding the Parade Service, it is important to note that British society at the start of the conflict was generally more involved in church life and Christianity. Between 25 and 29 percent of people attended church every Sunday and 90 percent of children attended Sunday school.

After only eleven days at Bordon Camp, Herbert would have received the news of the painful loss of his brother from illness. We do not know the effect this had, but he would surely have been devastated as he was very close to his siblings.

Herbert continued his work at the army camps in the Aldershot area and on 6 May 1915,[12] the Wesleyan Committee Meeting Minutes at Bordon Camp reported: "The committee regretted to hear of the probable removal of Mr Cowl, through the call of active service."

Herbert was initially assigned to the 9th (Scottish) Division of the British Army, a formation comprising Scottish battalions. On the 8 May 1915, the 9th (Scottish) Division began its move to France. However, the hierarchy of the Army and Navy Board in the Wesleyan Methodist church and the Army Chaplains' Department (AChD) considered that as a Wesleyan Army Chaplain, Herbert would be more suited to a division which would have had a higher proportion of Wesleyans in its component brigades, so he remained in England before receipt of his next instructions to join the 23rd (New Army) Division.[13] Most young Army Chaplains worked on the home front for a prolonged period of time before they were sent overseas. However, it would appear that in Herbert's case they identified an innate quality and suitability in him for Army Chaplaincy that his name was soon put forward for active service.

On Wednesday, 12th May, the *Western Daily Press* reported on a meeting that had taken place at the Wesleyan Methodist Synod in Bristol:

12   MARC, Minutes of Bordon Soldiers' Home Committee of Management & Trustees Meetings, September 1904 to December 1938.
13   MARC, Minutes Armed Forces Board 1915.

Attired in khaki, Mr Cowl rose, and soon brought the Synod face to face with the camp and the battlefield. Speaking from his experience of work in camp, he said the chaplain found two problems, first the problem of men who have come from their home churches, and are only traditionally attached to Christ, secondly the case of men who by former habits of life had no regard for religion. The great need was to strengthen the former and to save the latter. Mr Cowl emphasised the need of spiritual work in the institutes worked by the churches, and his address was listened to with rapt attention.[14]

It was recorded in the Wesleyan Methodist Conference Minutes in 1915:

Immediately after the commencement of hostilities the British Expeditionary Force was prepared for despatch to the theatre of operations. The War Office asked for the services of four Wesleyan Chaplains. The establishment of Wesleyan Chaplains with the Expeditionary Force in France and Flanders has since been increased to thirty-two.

Also in the same minutes there is comment on 'Spiritual and Moral Work':

There can be no question that the call to arms has afforded a unique opportunity for influencing the good, the flower of Britain's young manhood, which has heard and responded to the call. Whilst provision has been made to meet the social needs of young men, away from the restraints of home, living in a new environment, and exposed to great perils, their spiritual and moral needs have not been overlooked.

On 2nd June, Herbert signed the official papers regarding 'Acting Chaplains engaged for duty with the Expeditionary Force'. The document was witnessed by his colleague and friend, Congregational Army Chaplain, the Rev. Arthur Farrington C.F. and the paper was signed by A C Strange on behalf of the Secretary of State. In effect, this was Herbert's contract of employment for the duration of the war years.

On 26th June, Herbert was examined at West Chevin, Bournemouth and considered to be in a 'fit state of health' for service abroad.[15] Four days later, he wrote to the War Office informing them: 'I beg to state that my next of kin is: Rev. F.B. Cowl, Hampreston Manor Farm, Wimborne'.[16] Herbert knew that this was not his father's home address, but if anything should happen, it would be better for any foreboding news to be sent to his sister's address so that she could inform their mother and father in person. By late June, Herbert and Muriel's parents had moved from their previous

14   *Western Daily Press*, 12 May 1915.
15   The National Archives (TNA) WO 339/47342.
16   Ibid.

Acting Chaplains engaged for duty with Expeditionary Force.

Clergy.
Gen. No
4044

TO HIS MAJESTY'S PRINCIPAL SECRETARY OF STATE FOR THE WAR DEPARTMENT.

I, (name) *Herbert Butler Cowl.*

of (address) *"Brantfell" Whitehill Bordon*

Insert religious denomination.

being a duly ordained {priest / minister} of the *Wesleyan Church* .
hereby offer, and agree if accepted by you, to serve at home or abroad as a temporary Chaplain to His Majesty's Forces, 4th Class, with the relative rank of Captain in the Army while so employed, on the following conditions :—

1. The period of my service hereunder shall commence as from the day on which I shall commence duty, and shall continue until the expiration of 12 calendar months thereafter, or until my services are no longer required, whichever shall first happen.

2. My pay and allowances shall (subject as hereinafter appears) be at the rate authorized for 4th Class Chaplains to the Forces. (The pay is 10s. a day, and the allowances vary according to circumstances.)

3. In addition to such pay, I shall receive a free passage to any country abroad to which I may be sent, and (subject as hereinafter appears) a similar free passage back to England.

4. I shall receive free rations while in the field, and when considered necessary for the performance of my duties, the use of a Government horse and forage.

5. During the said period I will devote my whole time and energies to my service hereunder, and will obey all orders given to me by superior Military or Naval Officers.

6. In case I shall have completed my service hereunder to your satisfaction in all respects, I shall receive at the end of the said period a gratuity of 60 days' full pay at the rate hereinbefore specified, but in case I shall in any manner misconduct myself, or shall be (otherwise than through illness or unavoidable accident) unfit in any respect for service hereunder, of which misconduct or unfitness you or your authorized representative shall be sole judge, you shall be at liberty from and immediately after such misconduct or unfitness to discharge me from further service hereunder, and thereupon all pay and allowances shall cease, and I shall not be entitled to any free passage home or gratuity.

Dated this *Second* day of *June* 19 *15* .

H B Cowl. (Here sign.)

Witness to the signature of the said *H. B. Cowl.*

Arthur Farrington. C.F. (Witness.)

On behalf of the Secretary of State I accept the foregoing offer.

al strange

3 46) W 1859—1058 1000 4/15 H W V(P)

Herbert's Army Chaplain contract: A second copy was placed in his file which now resides at The National Archives (Kew) with his service record. (Author's collection)

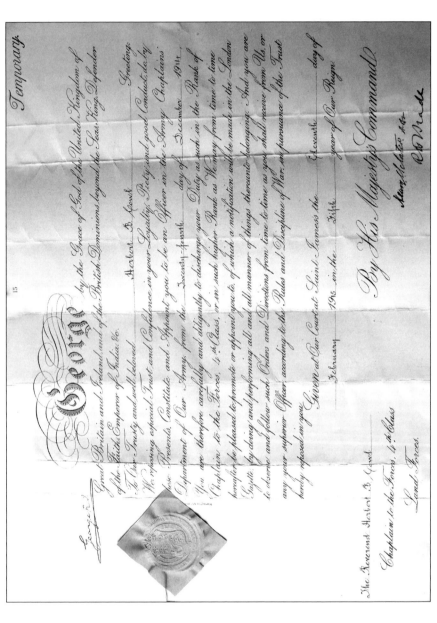

George by the Grace of God of the United Kingdom of Great Britain and Ireland …": Herbert's officer commission. (Author's collection)

OFFICERS. BATHING PARADE.

Herbert (second from left) with fellow officers; date and location unknown.
(Author's collection)

circuit in Llandudno, Conwy, North Wales to their new circuit, Birmingham (Sutton Park) and their new home was located in Anchorage Road, Sutton Coldfield, Warwickshire.

At the end of July, Herbert was still at Bordon Camp but soon after receiving his orders to begin his journey to the battlefields. He was transferred to the 68th Brigade of the 23rd Division which had been formed as part of Kitchener's Third New Army. On 27 July 1915, the 68th Brigade completed their first course of musketry at Bramshott Camp, near Haslemere. The Northumberland Fusiliers' regimental journal, *St. George's Gazette* reported on the final Inter-Battalion competition at Great Dene Range in Longmoor which comprised of 'firing 500 yards, five rounds being fired rapid and five deliberate'. The report also described the scenery as being 'delightful, and the country admirably adapted for military training'.[17]

Commissioned officers were allocated a batman (often referred to as an 'orderly'), a personal servant who would carry out many tasks including; acting as a valet looking after an officer's kit, carrying out the duties of 'runner' and various other miscellaneous duties. Some of the Army Chaplains who were offered such services enjoyed the benefits but, although we are uncertain whether or not Herbert was presented with

17   *St. George's Gazette*, 31 July 1915.

Outside Brantfell in Whitehill where
Herbert was living whilst at Bordon
Camp in the summer of 1915: family
visit prior to departure for France.
(Author's collection)

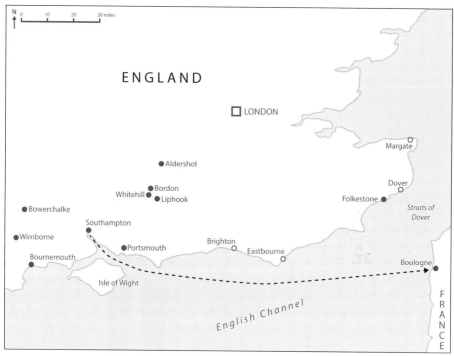

Map A Crossing the Channel. (George Anderson)

a personal servant, we do know that he never took advantage of the offer. However, later in the war, it is known that Herbert did share some of the benefits of the doctors' batmen whilst he was serving in Flanders.

On the morning of 24 August 1915, Herbert marched out of the temporary camp at Bramshott, with the men of the 68th Brigade, ready to serve as 'an Army Chaplain to His Majesty's Forces' at the front.[18] In the early hours of the morning, five trains left Liphook Station heading south towards Southampton Docks on their way to France. The following morning the sea was calm as the heavily-laden troopships crossed the English Channel to Boulogne. Accompanied by a destroyer in anticipation of German submarines, the convoy proceeded without any hostile action from the enemy. Their passage in the silence of night had been peaceful and quiet despite their possible pre-occupied thoughts of danger.[19]

18   TNA WO 95/2181/1.
19   *Oldham Chronicle*, 2 October 1915.

Formal photograph of Rev.
Captain H.B. Cowl C.F.
Bristol, December 1914.
(Author's collection)

Herbert was to remain with the 68th Brigade for the remainder of his war experiences in France and Belgium.[20] Comprised mainly of men from the northeast of
England, Methodist Churches in the region had been very well attended so it was a
natural choice to attach a Wesleyan padre to the brigade.

Now on the mainland of France, Herbert began to write home to his parents,
sharing with them the experiences and impressions of his war, the Great War. A war
like no other and one whereby he, the 'Padre', would be tested as a young Methodist
minister striving to make his mark as an Army Chaplain trying to impart the strength
and love of his faith with those around him.

He signed his letters to home, 'From your loving son, The Half-Shilling Curate,
Herbert'.

20   Ibid.

3

Early days in France

The 68th Brigade (GOC[1] Brigadier-General E. Pearce) of 23rd Division (GOC Major-General J.M. Babington) was raised during the autumn of 1914. Men were recruited from across the north-east of England for component infantry units – 10th and 11th battalions of the Northumberland Fusiliers (NF) and 12th and 13th battalions of the Durham Light Infantry (DLI) in Newcastle (each battalion comprising approximately 1,000 men). The north-east was an industrial powerhouse, highly populated in County Durham and parts of Northumberland, with many areas of labour intense industry including coal mining and ship building. It was an ideal source for strong eager young recruits wishing to join Kitchener's Army; to escape the harsh living conditions of the industrial north. Their journey to the Western Front began with training in various military camps in the south of England, which would eventually transform them from inexperienced recruits into soldiers.

The 68th Brigade included four Army Chaplains who embarked with the unit to France in late August 1915.[2] They were: Senior Chaplain the Rev. John Nelson Blakiston (Church of England) aged 36, and Chaplains, the Rev. Francis Temple Picton-Warlow (Church of England) aged 38, the Rev. Father Godric Kean (Roman Catholic)[3] aged 49 and Herbert, the 28 year old fresh-faced Wesleyan Army Chaplain. At the beginning of 1915, the Rev. Blakiston had been acting Chaplain for the 13th Durham Light Infantry at their home camp, but by August he was promoted to Senior Chaplain for the Brigade, it was Captain the Rev. Herbert B. Cowl who took his place.

Disembarking in France, there was no grand reception or celebration for the 68th Brigade, no public rejoicing or acknowledgement of their arrival, no tossed garlands or flowers, just bare cobbled streets and the prospect of a lengthy trek to the nearest basecamp. It was obvious that thousands of soldiers had marched through their town

---

1   GOC: General Officer Commanding.
2   TNA WO 95/2181/1.
3   The only brigade Army chaplain who came from north-east England.

Group photograph of the officers of the 13th Durham Light Infantry, March 1915.
Back row: Second Lieutenant W.A.L. Dray Cooper; Second Lieutenant Start; Second
Lieutenant E.A. Pullen; Second Lieutenant Geach; Second Lieutenant D.M. Clarke; Second
Lieutenant W.A.O. Read; Second Lieutenant Cooper; Second Lieutenant G. Butterworth;
Second Lieutenant J.G.M. Bell Middle row: Lieutenant P. A. Brown; Second Lieutenant
Oliphant; Lieutenant E.A.P. Wood; Captain E.A. Bellamy; Second- Lieutenant L.M.
Greenwood; Lieutenant L.M. Long; Lieutenant S.Q.M. Snow; Second- Lieutenant
Saverbeck; Lieutenant N.A. Target; Captain W. Miles; Lieutenant Jardine, Royal Army
Medical Corps; Second Lieutenant C.G. Hancock T.O. [Transport Officer] Front row:
Lieutenant H.L. Markham; Captain Blakiston, Chaplain of the Forces (before his promotion
to Senior Chaplain of the Brigade in the summer of 1915); Captain W.A.L. Downey;
Captain U.S. Naylor; Colonel G.A. Ashby C.B.[?]; Lieutenant E. Borrow, Adjutant; Captain
H. Austin; Captain Blake and Second Lieutenant Howard. (John Sheen)

in the previous weeks, months and year. The almost daily arrival of British troops had
become routine for the inhabitants of Boulogne with thousands of Tommies having
marched down their thoroughfares since the start of the conflict.

The crossing had passed without incident; the weather was fine and it could not
have been a more perfect summer day when the transport ships docked in the harbour
before dawn at approximately 4:00 a.m. on the 26th August. Herbert had arrived in
France with an uncertain future ahead.

On arrival in Boulogne, the four battalions of the 68th Brigade proceeded towards Ostrohove Camp near the town's outskirts.[4] Herbert, as a commissioned officer, would have been billeted at brigade headquarters with fellow chaplains. The men of his battalion would have been billeted in tented camps. During these early days, the 13th Battalion DLI's full complement consisted of 31 officers (including musician and composer George Butterworth), a medical officer, chaplain (Herbert) and 939 other ranks. Everything was new and exciting, boisterous singing and much jollity following disembarkation. For the majority, it was the first opportunity to experience an overseas adventure as most of them would never have left England before this war.

Herbert's first letter home was written the day after his arrival in France – the stated location being detailed as the well-known adage 'Somewhere in France'. It has a relaxed tone of someone whose adventure is just beginning:

Beloved Little Mother,
Behold me established in the cool, roomy bedroom of the Village Mayor! Outside, a shady garden of fruit trees and vegetables, beyond which the beautiful and peaceful country stretches away up to the firing line:- which is just out of earshot; thou mine host M. le Maire has been trying to explain to me that the other day they heard the 'boom boom' (with much brandishing of arms) of the big guns. It is a beautiful village with 2 or 3 peasant inns, at one of which I grub. French bread and butter are excellent. Not much else!

M. le M speaks no word of English, nor do my good friends at the inn. But my school days have returned to my help and I have already interpreted for a number of stranded comrades, besides delighting the inhabitants myself!

We had a glorious crossing, in radiant moonlight and an unruffled sea. Our first night, of some 4 hours was spent in a big canvas camp on a hill overlooking xxx [Boulogne] and the sea. No blanket, no 'biscuit' [mattress], so HBC took unkindly to hard mother earth and heard most that transpired thro' those few long hours.

The 68th Brigade spent its first night at the camp overlooking Boulogne. The following day the men marched to the railway station. Transported by cattle trucks (40 men in each), the officers travelled in more comfortable carriages. The train was very long – it also transported the wagons and horses of the brigade transport. It took them approximately 28 miles east to St Omer (BEF headquarters) where they set up camp for their second night on the Western Front.[5] Split into four camps approximately five miles north-west of Saint-Omer at Houlle, Ganspette, Eperlecques and Moulle, the battalions settled in. Herbert and the other officers were billeted in the nearby village of Houlle. No doubt the men

4   TNA WO 95/2182/2.
5   WO 95/2182/1.

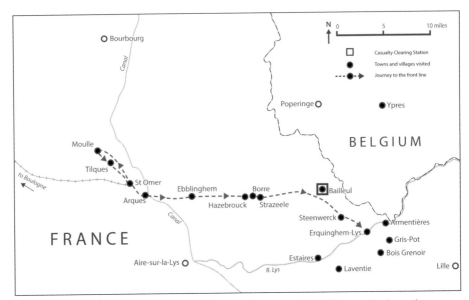

Map B Journey to the front, summer and autumn 1915. (George Anderson)

would have enjoyed their first days in France, appreciating the sights and sounds of peaceful little French villages, seemingly untouched communities with local life continuing much as usual, almost as if there was no war apart from the fact that there were hundreds and thousands of soldiers deployed in the region, waiting for instruction to move to the front. The countryside around Boulogne would have been beautiful and untouched by the war, sweeping green landscape with the highest tips of towers and church spires showing through the trees. The splendid, tranquil and occasionally scarred chateaux and monasteries would have been a reminder of a troubled history these provinces had experienced many centuries earlier:

> A hot and dusty morning march took us to our train. I wish you could have seen and heard us, swinging thro' those old world villages to the strains of 'till the boys come home'. But oh! These packs!! Mine must total with ruck sack on back, Burberry beneath it, haversack one side, water bottle the other, all chock full – some 100 lbs. But I wasn't too done to carry sometimes two rifles for lads who were falling out.
>
> At my inn I am accosted by a French Red X private: he, in broken English, – "you are a clergy man sir?" "yes." "Are you Roman Catholic?" "No." "I am sorry: I am a priest!" "But we love you all the same!" "Très bien!" and we shake hands heartily.
>
> In the old, rambling house of a fat French woman I find myself seeking fruit for sale; great luscious pears at 1d [one old penny] each. – I carry on a long and

imperfect conversation; during which I am introduced – "Monsieur le Capitaine!" – to most, if not all her relatives and I depart well laden.

M. le M retires at 9.30 and HBC rises at 7.30. So after fruitless efforts to explain to mine host that my appearance in the morning is a memorable feast, I retire with, "Je ne sais pas. Je vais me coucher!" and enjoy a long refreshing night from which I have wakened, better than ever for the fatigue of yesterday. I cannot tell you more, but will write when I can find time.

Herbert concluded with a few practicalities ('Little Super' being an affectionate term of endearment – a shortened name he often used for his father who was a 'Superintendent' Minister,[6] responsible for his designated circuit, which at this time was Sutton Coldfield in Warwickshire):

God go with you! I will send a list of modest requirements to Mukie shortly, when I am more certain of postal arrangements. But letters will find me at 68th Infantry Brigade Headquarters. Will Mukie please keep careful account of all I ask her and I will repay her in due course.

Best of best love to you and the Little Super!

In those first few days in France, the men of 68th Brigade enjoyed some fine weather. Persistent rain followed in September. The Brigade was dispatched on various training programmes which included divisional tactical exercises in the area of Serques, a machine gun course and separate instruction on the use and manufacture of bombs.[7] Trench familiarisation began under the tutelage of the 20th (Light) Division and the 27th (Regular) Division.

Herbert the chaplain wearing shorts – date and location unknown. (Author's collection)

6   An elder minister who serves in a supervisory position over a geographic "district" of churches.
7   WO 95/2182/1.

A few days later, after receiving mail from home, Herbert eagerly wrote back to his mother and father from a tiny village inn – his temporary billet:

Beloved Little People,
I have today received two letters from you – a great joy, I can assure you!

Would you please send me a skein of brown wool (about khaki) for darning socks, and a darning needle. Also, would you please write to the man who advertised Manse Socks in the Recorder [Methodist Recorder]. I ordered and paid for three pairs: he answered that owing to many orders he could not yet send them. Would you please ask him to send them to you. Then you can send them here when I am ready for them.

Our 'open-air café' has today been swamped right out – awful weather: never saw worse. So, we (the Doctor, Quartermaster and I) have moved to a new quarters, the end of a passage in the tiny village school! It is very dingy there, but it has the virtue of dryness, and we have resurrected a table from no one knows where! Dinner today, steak, potatoes, carrots and onions: figs, cheese, and as much of all as one could eat! All off one plate, of course. Also, one cup serves for the three of us. But our meals are a triumph. And all absolutely free! Sometimes I buy eggs, or French bread for a change. But besides such incidental luxuries there is no expense – praise be!

Our battalion officers are noted for snobbery and I think not wrongly so. The Quartermaster (full lieutenant, in rank) is a 'ranker', and is rigidly excluded for that unfordonable offence!!

The Doctor is my special chum; he and I 'hit it' grandly so far. He is a real Scotchman: very quiet and deliberate, reserved and capable; has been married for one year, but in practice for several. Every day after dinner I retire to his billet for 'café noir' and a quiet smoke with him. Here we successfully rectify the faults of the universe in general and the battalion in particular. It is a great mercy to find a friend. I always need them. And God in his giving has never yet failed me in this respect: for which I record my gratitude.

The battalion is not fighting yet. I am.

It is all very, very different from anything yet that has come my way. And it is strange indeed how we all fret to be right up there where we can hear the low grumble of the angry guns.

Sometimes as I cross a bit of rising ground between here and Headquarters, where the country is open, and the road only lined by an endless avenue of huge polled witch-elms, I stand in the darkness; watch the probing searchlights flicker on to the clouds and hear those grim far off voices speaking death. It is a new sound; it is another world; and it calls to unprecedented scenes and experiences. God grant as we march into it all, that there may arise a man in me that is sufficient to this new occasion!

Men of 71st Field Ambulance in camp shortly after enlistment. (Author's collection)

During the coming weeks, various ancillary units re-joined the 68th Brigade, including battalion transport sections and the 71st Field Ambulance.[8] On Sunday, 5th September orders were received for brigade manoeuvres the following day, and on the 6th, the men were ready to move onwards to Hazebrouck – a twenty-three mile eastward march to their next encampment. Their subsequent route passed through Tilques, St Martin au Laert, Arques, and Ebblinghem. The silence of picturesque landscape would have been shattered by the din of large numbers of men marching through the countryside, along with the pounding hooves of newly-shod horses, the creaking sound of heavily loaded wooden General Service (GS) waggons, the rhythmic hum of motor transport and the distant rumble of heavy artillery.

The weather as described in the 68th Brigade's war diary 'was fine and warm but not oppressive'. The march would have been a physical challenge for the fittest of men as they advanced through the cobbled streets of the French villages and towns, so strange to them, and along straight dusty, long roads stretching for miles ahead, with only the occasional shade provided by avenues lined with plane trees. The men were no doubt exhausted by the end of their march. The tranquillity of the flat pictur-esque countryside would change as they moved east, nearer to the front, closer to the theatre of war. Villages and farms displayed scars of previous bombardments. The

8   TNA WO 95/2179/3.

architecture changed as they moved towards Belgium. The soldiers were approaching the front line – only twenty-four miles to the front trenches.

Herbert's next letter home described the strenuous marching which gives a true indication of how very strong he was both mentally and physically! His stamina was an early indication of the respect he was to earn from his men whilst on active service:

> … the 'bloated aristocracy' of fighting men who go to war on four legs instead of two? Ah well, the horse is a noble animal, I am sure: but it was my lot to journey with the humbler class of 'toe-busters'. No one knows why we did it: but we made two record marches: and who could forget the longer of the two – twenty-three miles on French roads, under a blazing September Sun, and with full pack and ammunition. (No, the Padre does not carry ammunition, but I managed to appropriate two or three rifles to make up the deficiency.) From my place at the rear of the battalion where I marched with the Doctor, I watched my friend the Sergeant, tugging at his load: his fellow Sergeant gave in and fell in a heap in the road-side ditch: but he would not give in though his men dropped in handfuls towards the end: nor would he yield his rifle to me even for a few yards. Hard things are said of man, and of God, at such times, when men only keep their feet by sheer weight of will-power.

Arriving in Hazebrouck, assigned billets were overcrowded due to a misunderstanding between French and British authorities. To add to the confusion, the supply wagons did not arrive until midnight.[9] Herbert observed:

> Beloved Little People,
> Imagine us parading in the early hours of the morning and swinging off in a cool breeze, a well damped road and a radiant sun. The Doc. and I with his stretcher bearers bring up the rear.
> That was my first day's real soldiering for we marched 22 miles in full pack and with only one serious halt of one hour. The roads were awful: great square cobbles in the centre, with often rough stones each side. It pulled the men about fiercely: but I was delighted – being the son of my father – to finish up fresh as the freshest, despite two rifles for the last six to eight miles.
> The night that followed – ne parlez pas! A tile floor: a bundle of straw; a Burberry for warmth and HBC got to sleep at 4.45 am and rose at 5.15 am. The night had been passing cold: but the day proved to be surpassing hot. So that the 12 miles added to our sojourn were about the wickedest bit of work yet. If old England could have seen her fallen sons by the road-side and her unfallen ones staggering along in the sweltering heat – well old England would turn in her complaisant sleep and dream some!

9   TNA WO 95/2181/1.

Sometimes I was slung up with three rifles, 'till the owners would take them back and crawl into the nearest ditch. Well, it has been a fierce day and the stiffest bit of pulling I have yet done, despite all my travels: but I think I have won a little respect at least in the battalion – a necessary victory!

At 9:00 a.m. on the following day, Tuesday 7th September, the 68th Brigade left Hazebrouck for Steenwerck – a march of approximately thirteen miles. This time the journey took them along the main road through Borre, Strazeele and Bailleul. The weather was extremely hot and many men were recorded as having 'fallen out' of the march, as a result of the blazing sun, the rough cobbled roads and the unbearable weight of their large packs.

That evening Herbert wrote of his new accommodation:

The Doc. and I now mess with The Colonel, the 2nd in command and the Adjutant – not so free and easy company as before but we shall fit in all right. I think Col. said last night that he was not going to have us switched off to the Field Ambulance – 'some talk' if you knew him!

This is a sweet, peaceful spot, five miles from the firing line! Half-a-dozen planes were fighting a Zep [Zeppelin] just above the trees last night – the only sign of war we have seen.

The kitchen floor is made of quite solid stone, upon which the Doc and I slept on our valises. I slept like a top most of the night – until Madame, Mlle, etc etc entered and continued a steady procession to and fro! This is a fine old farm, with 1100 fowls, acres of haricot beans and I don't know what else. But we are not here for long – enough said.

More often than not, he would add a request at the bottom of his correspondence. On this occasion: 'Please ask Mukie to get me – Boracic: Sterilisers; Phenacetin and Horlicks.' Phenacetin was a well-known medicine of its time and was used to relieve pain and fever; Boracic was a powder used for small wounds to help healing and Horlicks were malted milk tablets.

On 8th September, the men of 12th and 13th DLI were inspected by Lieutenant-General Sir William Pulteney (GOC III Corps) to which the 23rd Division was attached.[10] The weather continued fine and warm and during the following week the 68th Brigade commenced trench warfare instruction. Divided into platoons, officers and men were dispatched to various sections of the line to undergo training with experienced battalions. This would have been their first experience as soldiers in a battle situation; it was at Laventie that 13th Battalion experienced their baptism of fire. Mixed with host unit platoons, trench duty instructions were related by experienced veterans before taking over part of the front line on their own. These were the

10   WO 95/2167/1.

final days of training before the 68th Brigade took full responsibility for assigned trench bays on the front line. Sadly, during the final days of this acclimation period, the Brigade suffered a number of casualties killed and wounded. Indeed, during the last week of September, the 68th Brigade's War diarist recorded three men killed and 27 wounded during the seven days of instruction. This was considered to be 'a rather high proportion considering the general quietude prevailing'. There were accidental deaths too, including one soldier who drowned whilst washing in the river at Estaires.

Although the 68th Brigade's component battalions were deemed to include a high proportion of Methodists, they also included men of all faiths and denominations. Nonetheless, Herbert would have looked after them all without prejudice or discrimination. At times services were even carried out by two or more chaplains (of different denomination) from the same rostrum.

As 68th Brigade neared its time of readiness, the high spirits indicative of early days in France and Flanders had all but died away; indeed a peculiar hush descended upon the men, a sense of apprehension and anticipation of battle. Despite this, Herbert managed to retain his bright positive disposition on life. Herbert's fellow Chaplain, the Rev. Father Godric Kean, the Roman Catholic priest, wrote home to his Oldham parishioners about the officers and men of 68th Brigade:

> The officers are men of skill, resource, and daring, and I consider no words of praise too great to be given to these excellent fellows drawn from every profession who, while they adorn the army by their high qualifications, strengthen it by their chivalrous conduct. I have seen them under every condition at home and across the seas. In the camp, on the march, in the trenches, they are always the same 'without fear and without reproach.'

Herbert's next letter home is dated 16th September:

> Mother Mine,
> First, thank you very much indeed, both of you, for your birthday greetings, and for the most useful gifts of hairbrush and collar and pin. Bless you!
> It was a strange birthday, which I forgot till night-time!
> Thus it passed: At 5.45 mine hostess brought me my Cawl of steaming café-au-lait and by breakfast (7.45) I had my 'roly-poly' packed and ready to 'move on' at mid-day. Just as we were about to start the Transport Officer was called away and the whole column of Transport and Details was put under the command of your redoubtable son! Imagine me marching at the head of about 20 infantrymen, nearly a dozen wagons of ammunition, etc. four pack ponies (with ammunition) and other oddments. My road was to be direct, about 3 miles; to a certain field by the wayside, near by a town which is only just un-bombarded. But, half a mile out, I was stopped by a French official, who directed me and my column another way, which added some four miles to our journey and very much heat and vigour to the oaths of my men with bad feet and other complaints!

However, I piloted them there; some awfully round-about roads right to the very spot – praise be!

Having handed them over to O.C. [Officer Commanding] details, I toddled off to choose a billet – in which I am now sitting. The Belgian refugees of whom there are about seven in the house! – have done my washing beautifully and darned my socks for the small sum, details of which I enclose for your amusement.

However, as relaxed as he appears in this correspondence, Herbert has obviously begun to experience some of the hardships of war, the details of which he does not share out of consideration for loved ones:

I'm living a quiet life just now. To bed between 9 and 9.30, up at 6. Eating more than ever before and generally enjoying life. My work is difficult, but I'm slowly getting track of it. There are 'many adversaries'.

The weather was now beginning to turn and the warm; dry sunny weather was replaced by rainfall and signs of the coming autumn and winter. Nevertheless, some warm days remained, as thousands of men appreciated the simple outdoor pleasures of washing and bathing.

Herbert's next letter describes his changing role with a closer affiliation with the Royal Army Medical Corps (RAMC). Attached to the 71st Field Ambulance,[11] this posting may not have been official until late September. The 71st had been based at Bordon Camp before departing for France on 26th August, so Herbert may have been acquainted with some of its personnel prior to their embarkation. The 71st Field Ambulance left England with a total strength of 10 officers and 219 other ranks:

Dearest Little People,

Sorry to be so long writing: that is the worst of writing often and much, that one cannot always get it done and a gap may seem ominous to you.

But you must be fully prepared sometimes to wait a long while for letters.

The men for whom I am responsible have this week taken over their part of the 'line!' and I have been busy getting track of them – a business indeed! If you want to know what aching muscles feel like, walk a couple of miles of trench, floored with a double row of planks which are thoroughly greasy with rain and clay. Sometimes you will take a turn, as a welcome relief, in the four to six inches of oozy mud that runs beside the planks. Meanwhile, you will bless the makers of Lotus boots and trust that the boy who cleans 'em tomorrow is gifted with patience and grit!

11   A mobile front line medical unit (not a vehicle) manned by Royal Army Medical Corps.

I had a strange day Sunday. Drove off in a Motor Ambulance (a habit I am eagerly falling into!!) to find some of my Battalions. In this I failed: but landed at last at Farrington's morning service for his ambulance in which I joined.

It is the Council Chamber, 2nd floor up, in a building gaunt, but better than most about it, which is not saying much. The street outside is cobbled right across and along it thunders up an incessant stream of limbers, gun carriages, transports, motors, etc. The three front windows look out upon this chaos. But the three at the other side of the room look far out over a long stretch of flat but pretty country, all aglow with the radiant morning sun. F. [Rev. Farrington] stands against the mid window.

As he preaches I notice three things: just over his head (though really six miles away) hangs a British captive balloon: and once high over it there circles a tiny speck – a Taube[12] – round which the white innocent-looking smoke flowers are bursting into bloom and drifting away, white and tiny, into the blue. They are the exploding shells of British anti-aircraft guns. Then on his left a group of nuns in a quaint old grave yard are bowed over an open grave. While on his right, half a dozen English Tommies are having the usual morning tussle with a bunch of refractory mules.

Amidst all this we sing the old familiar hymns: and F. gives us (almost 30) a good talk from the words, 'cleave to that which is good'.

I tramp back four miles to lunch. Then another Motor which takes me to the outskirts of xxx (ask Mukie she knows!). The car carries F. and me. It draws into the cover of a high wall – knowing the measure of the German regard for its badge! F. burrows into a large cellar to take Service and I link up with a young lieutenant who is jogging on a bit further, into the trenches.

Those houses that we pass are a strange sight, though they have been so often described. Here and there one can boast a whole pane of glass: often the door stands half open and shows all inside empty: perhaps a great gash in the wall: perhaps a whole wall swept away. And, then in the midst of a so grim row, there stands one curtained, cleaned and mended with big sheets of biscuit tin: inside, an array of chocolates, P.P.C.s [Picture Post Cards], nick-knacks, etc. and a handful of jolly kiddies romping about the door! I need not describe their perils: you will imagine them.

But, I am asking – '... and become as little children ... !', is there then something in the possession of the Kingdom of Heaven that gives the heart a 'carelessness' like that of these children? I think so. But I think I will be better able to say a week or two hence.

My first service comes when I get back to Hospital at Six. About 70 there. One of my old Bordon boys in the service sheds tears of joy as we grip hands afterwards.

---

12   Although a Taube was a specific make, British troops often referred to all German aircraft as Taubes.

This week I have had a Class Meeting,[13] with six present, here in my billet. But today my program changes slightly.

My boys are in the trenches and it is nine miles each way to them. So, I'm off on my own to join a lovely Doctor of the 69th F.A. – in a cellar! It's a fine place, safe as home, with its piles and piles of sandbags in case of any quite unforeseen emergency: and as I have told you, this is the quietest bit of all the line.

The 69th Field Ambulance, another component unit of 23rd Division, arrived in France via Le Havre aboard the S.S. *Empress Queen*.[14] It comprised 10 officers, 183 personnel, 38 Army Service Corps (ASC), 3 Ambulance wagons, 6 General Service wagons, 4 limber (two-wheeled) carts, 3 water carts, 1 cycle and 56 horses and mules.

Herbert continued with a request for some additional essentials:

By the way, I could do very well with a pair of really thick sleeping socks, I think: not white, or pink!! but a dark, strong and grisly pair! thick muffler khaki wool would be the best. I guess I shall not undress for a week or two now: but it is nice to change one's socks for the night.

Finally, he offered some reassurance and hope:

I'm having a good time: slowly getting the hang of things. If only (!!) the war will last long enough, I shall become quite a capable Chaplain, I can assure you! (But it will have to last long enough!!!) Best love to you both. Very many thanks for all letters: most welcome: never quite so much before, I think!

From your loving son …

The 23rd Division, now deployed in French Flanders, completed its period of trench warfare instruction. Tasked by III Corps of General Sir Douglas Haig's First Army to take sole responsibility for the Bois Grenier sector extending north as far as Armentières, its component units prepared for a front line composed primarily of breastworks[15] due to the low water table. The 68th Brigade's war diarist detailed the training programme:

… the artillery bombardment of enemy trenches commenced and continued all day. "Gas" experiments on officers and men carried out, without mishap, at Erquinghem – Lys.'[16] Four days later, poison gas was used by the BEF for the

13   A small group of soldiers who would pray together and possibly discuss spiritual matters with their chaplain.
14   TNA WO 95/2179/1.
15   Temporary fortification, often earthwork to breast height to provide protection to defenders firing over it from a standing position.
16   TNA WO 95/2181/1.

first time with devastating results at the Battle of Loos which commenced on 25 September 1915.

The Durham Battalions were tasked with providing working parties for the construction of strongpoints and trench improvement for the long winter ahead. They, along with the men of the Northumberland Fusiliers, were particularly adept at this task due to the majority of the men having been miners prior to enlistment.

Dearest Little Mother,

Will you first note that my address from now will be – '71st Field Ambulance B.E.F. France'. To continue the narrative from the time of conducting my column to their new bivouac; after three days we re-joined the battalion. Imagine my joy when I was informed that I was billeted in a farm with my good friend Dr McKerrow!

We occupied the 'large room' of a typical wayside farmhouse; barely within range of the German batteries. Dr had a bed in the corner of the room: I had a tiny bedroom opening out of it. And for three days we enjoyed to the full a happy comradeship.

On Sunday morning I had a fine parade service, with about 150 present. It was held in a field, with a fine east wind sweeping through our pillarless temple and a flood of sunlight. I had the men formed in three sides of a square; and I ordered them all to sit down while I 'preached'. I wish you could have seen them listen! I will not soon forget it. I did not give them a 'text' – but it would have been "To me to live is – ?" I do trust that some chose and some re-chose Christ.

In the afternoon the Dr and I walked into -----,[17] a town of some size that has recently been fairly heavily bombarded and from which I told you I saw the refugees evacuating. It was very quiet while we were there. Here and there a house was minus a few bricks, or scarred all over its face with shrapnel bursts: now and then sandbags took the place of panes of glass: but on the whole it was not so much of a wreck as the last firing-line town that I was in. We tramped 10 miles, and were not even so much as sniped at. This confirms what I think I told you before, that we are at present on about the quietest bit of front in all the line.

In the evening about 15 of us gathered in the corner of a field and squatted on the ground, we held our little service – one of those hallowed and quietly memorable times that one hopes for most.

I think I was just beginning to faintly make myself felt in the 10th, and in time would have found some place amongst them. But on Monday, came my orders to transfer to the Field Ambulance. This means that at present I am back 3 miles. Further from the firing line, well out of range. Here I am in a cosy little house,

17   All sensitive information including place names had to be omitted from letters due to wartime Army Postal Service censorship.

with an excellent bed-sitting room, as comfortable as a man could be. Our mess comprises nine doctors, the Quartermaster, and three padres, 1 C. of E., 1 R. C. and myself.

How long we shall be here I cannot say. It may be two days; it may be two years! I might explain that when a Brigade goes into action, its Field Ambulance splits into three sections – 1. Advanced Dressing Station; 2. Dressing Station; and 3. Rest Hospital. I shall be either at 1. or 2; I expect, at 1. It depends which gives me the best access to the most men and I can only find out by experience.

At present I am more or less busy 'making friends' with various oddments of men: a difficult but happy task and one in which I need for more training. But in the main, especially with such matchless weather, things have been so far a prolonged picnic.

In addition to his orders, Herbert would have received some guidance from the Wesleyan Methodist Church which assumed that, as an ordained Wesleyan minister, he would know exactly how to fulfil the assigned role and what his commissioned responsibilities were as a Wesleyan Army Chaplain. Indeed, Herbert knew that his primary role was the welfare of the men – to care for their souls in the form of offering comfort and solace accompanied by sound Christian guidance. Although, at times there may have been mixed messages coming from both the army and the church – possibly conflict at times and perhaps on other occasions no instructions at all. Undoubtedly there would have been moments when the ecclesiastical authorities and the War Office would have agreed or disagreed depending on prevailing wartime

Hazebrouck c.1915. (Author's collection)

circumstances. It is also important to remember that whilst at Bordon, Herbert had signed official paperwork for 'Acting Chaplains engaged for duty with Expeditionary Force', whereby as an Army Chaplain he had agreed to: 'obey all orders given to me by superior Military or Naval Officers'. However, it was during those autumnal days of 1915, we can discern from Herbert's early correspondence that it was very much a matter of 'muddling through'. Certainly, in those first days and weeks in France, there would have been situations when he would have had to use his initiative and act as he thought best. There was no fixed programme – the work was infinitely varied and never-ending. Fundamentally though, Herbert learned that his full concentration needed to be focused on not only the spiritual, moral and mental, but also the physical and medical needs of the men he was assigned to serve. Like so many other Army Chaplains, he would discover that his work would become critical in maintaining a high level of general morale within the Army.

Herbert's role was destined to change as he moved closer to the front. In addition to attending to the living and wounded, the dead were to be identified and recorded. Corpses would be searched for personal items prior to burial services in officially designated cemeteries. A long winter in the trenches lay ahead, but Herbert's life was destined to take a more dangerous and unexpected turn during the coming months.

Armentières c.1915. (Author's collection)

4

Life in French Flanders

___

The weather on Saturday 25 September 1915 was cloudy with heavy rain and a south-westerly wind arrived later in the day. A General Headquarters message, forwarded by Brigade H.Q. was received by the 13th DLI Headquarters at 1:00 a.m. It read as follows:

> Chief wishes troops to be informed that he feels confident they will realise how much our success in the forthcoming operations depends on the individual efforts of each officer, N.C.O. and man. He wishes this to be conveyed to them verbally in such a manner as not to disclose our intentions to the enemy.

At approximately 4:20 a.m., a wire was received from the 68th Brigade which read: 'Rouse your men and get them fed.'

Later at close to 8:10 a.m., a second message from 68th Brigade disclosed the result of a diversionary attack at Bois Grenier:[1] 'Enemy reported to be surrendering fairly freely. Two battalions 8th Division reported in German 3rd line trenches.' The message would later prove to be false; 8th (Regular) Division's narrow-front assault was subsequently repulsed with heavy losses.

These messages were the first tangible sign of a major Allied offensive (25 September – 15 October 1915) extending from Arras to La Bassée – the opening day of a major Anglo-French push of which the Battle of Loos was the primary British effort. Notable for the BEF's first use of poison gas, albeit with mixed results (many British soldiers were incapacitated when the wind direction changed), combined British casualties amounted to 50,380 killed, wounded and missing before the stalemate settled in again. (Total British casualties to this point in the war were over 512,000, of which some 200,000 were killed or missing in action.)[2]

---

1   TNA WO 95/2181/1.
2   *Awarded for Valour: A History of the Victoria Cross and the Evolution of British Heroism* (UK: Palgrave Macmillan, 2008) pp.137.

The 23rd Division participated in divisionary efforts to support the British offensive, including smoke candle discharge along the divisional front.[3] Herbert, although not directly involved in these 'draw show' operations, would have carried on with his varied duties. However, he would have been aware that something major was going on further down the line, but at this stage he wouldn't have fully understood the extent of the great battle taking place some miles to the south. During the Battle of Loos, the 23rd Division were responsible for holding the front in the Bois Grenier sector. Although they were not directly involved in the battle, the 68th Brigade continued their operations and the 69th and 71st Field Ambulances dealt with casualties throughout the period.

Two days into the Battle of Loos, Herbert wrote home and, as usual, conveyed a positive outlook with only the slightest indication that he might be in a more dangerous situation than he was letting on!

> Mother Mine,
> Post-time is joy-time these days! And your letter received 10 minutes ago broke a long spell of monotony with a thrill of joy.
> You have no need to lie awake over this child, my dear little mother! I am quite as safe as you are! We are lying 8 miles behind what is reputed the quietest and securest part of all the Western Front. And (more's the pity!) little prospect of leaving it!
> Our Ambulance has formed the 'Divisional Rest Camp', which means that we get all the cases of easily curable sickness and slight wounds. This makes my position rather incongruous. We were attached to the Ambulance because it was considered the most central position from which to reach the whole of our Brigade. As it turns out at present, my Brigade is – no one knows where; but probably 10 or 15 miles from here!

In the same correspondence, Herbert writes with more incidental detail concerning colleagues in the 68th Brigade and the Field Ambulances. It is not known exactly when, but he was transferred to 69th Field Ambulance maintaining his role as Army Chaplain to the DLI and NF battalions.

We know that in the middle of September, the 69th Field Ambulance had taken over medical responsibility for a large area including the whole Bois Grenier sector. At the end of September, the main dressing station was situated at Fort Rompu, a disused brewery. The War Diary detailed that they were dealing with 27 wounded soldiers and 18 men who were described as 'sick'. In Herbert's next letter, one almost has the impression that he was writing about anything but the truth in terms of the grim reality of the war going on around him:

3   TNA WO 95/2167/1.

I am now quite out of touch with Dr McKerrow. He is a Battalion Doctor and remains exclusively with the Battalion.

Let me describe a little of our Mess. First, (but far from foremost!) are the 3 padres, – Father Kean, R.C., Picton-Warlow, C. of E., H.B.C., 'O.C. Details'! Kean is a jolly little old man: short, fat, bald, what hair is left, grey to white. Very genial and very rightly named after the manner of the typical Romanist. Warlow is a sallow, long-faced Welshman: impresses you as being both fierce and gloomy: but improves slightly on acquaintance. Both are kindly and tolerant, if a little patronising toward the 3rd member of this worthy group of clergy!

However, the Rev. Father Godric Kean was beginning to develop a respect for his Wesleyan counterpart and in a letter home to Oldham he wrote:

The spirit of self-sacrifice and a readiness to oblige seems to prevail in the army more than civilian life. A young Wesleyan Chaplain [Herbert] to save me a journey, undertook to see that the necessary arrangements for mass to be said to some Catholic troops, who were temporarily without a Chaplain, at a place which I could not reach myself in time to make the arrangements. [sic] Everything falls subservient to the spiritual and temporal welfare of our men.[4]

From the previous correspondence, Herbert continued with a description of the other members of his mess:

The C.O., Major Pooley (I think he spells himself thus) is a quiet and placid old gentleman, an old army doctor, tells long and wearisome stories, which evoke peals of laughter – from himself. The Adjutant is Capt. Picken, a short, smart, refined little Scotch Dr, Very Scottish; a teetotaller (of more consistent teeto-talism than the Major, who professes the same.) He is a Presbyterian and is very decent to me.

Lieut. Dryer (Dr), the Transport Officer is the son of a South African farmer and a Unitarian. There is one Lieut. Bramwell, the great great grandson of none other than the famous old Methodist Preacher William Bramwell!! But please don't suggest to him that he has any other connection with Methodism unless you wish to be withered!

My two best friends are Morron and Forester. Morron is the one who came to my service at Bordon and of whom I told you formerly. He is a jolly rollicking fellow: the life of the Mess at times and a good friend, in a rather non-committal way, to me. Forester is a quiet reserved Scotchman, very 'dour', but a jolly good fellow and one who I believe would do anything for me in my work. I go to their billet most evenings after Mess and we have some grand yarns. The Quartermaster (the only non-medical member) is a very short, shrewd, jolly cockney regular: just what you expect of the Q.M.!

Herbert ended this letter with some general observations of life at the front:

I must not describe more. As regards Services – my open-air parades follow just the same order of service as an indoor service and singing a foremost part and goes well. I am sorry that I cannot tell you anything about 'other Battalions': all information as to disposition of troops is strictly 'defend'. When I come home I will explain many things. Leave is due – if practicable, after three months of Active Service.

I should much like the Recorder. Who is the second of our Chaplains to be wounded? I heard of Harris, but not one since. You need not worry: I might be continents from war at present. On the other side of the road stands an old Convent, the bell of which is languidly tolling: children laugh and gambol in the street. I jog along, seeking something to do and often in vain! Nothing could be more unlike war! Last night I gave a Service for the RAMC [Royal Army Medical Corps] men and some patients in the 'Hospital' (the town school) dining hall. Had the C.O., 2 Drs, and about 80 men there. A good time, on the whole.

His most indelible memory of this period was written after the war when he described the moment he recognised one of the dishevelled soldiers returning from the Battle of Loos, Joe Foster, a private in the 8th Black Watch – a Highland regiment whom he had known at Bordon Camp:

It was they who took and lost and took again the Hohenzollern Redoubt at the Battle of Loos: and at the roll call after that holocaust, he was one of 115 who answered. They went in eleven hundred strong! They were in again a few weeks after: and yet again, till as a battalion they have ceased to exist: but Joe is still whole and well, I am told. And may God bring him safe and honoured through it all!

Herbert was to see 'Joe' one last time. Joe had told the Rev. H.B. Cowl that he was sure he would come through the war unscathed and this he did:

I saw him last in Laventie. His division had pulled out of the Battle of Loos mauled and decimated. I chanced to be in the streets of the broken town as the remnants marched through and there at the back of a gun carriage, Joe Foster racing along in his kilt. I broke all military discipline and pushed into the column to grip his hand and go with him while we talked.

On 29 September 1915 a 'Special Order of the Day' was sent from Secretary of State for War Field-Marshal Right Hon. H.H. Earl Kitchener of Khartoum to the Field-Marshal Commanding-in-Chief, Sir John French prior to circulation throughout the BEF including 23rd Division Headquarters:

> My warmest congratulations to you and all serving under you on the substantial success you have achieved and my best wishes for the progress of your important operations.
>
> Signed, Kitchener[5]

By late September, the rain continued and the weather was beginning to turn unsettled and cold. The clay-like mud affected everyone – with many roads turned into canals of sludge and meadows transformed into lagoons. Meanwhile, the battalions of the 68th Brigade, now in reserve, were billeted in villages in the immediate vicinity. There were constant casualties in all the battalions as men engaged with the enemy across their sector of the front line.

At the beginning of October, Herbert met Dr Phillip Gosse[6] of the RAMC who was carrying out his medical duties with the 69th Field Ambulance. Herbert wanted to help, (to provide moral support and comfort to the wounded and sick) so he used his initiative to ask if he could be put to use in the Advanced Dressing Station (ADS) working alongside the doctor. Dr Gosse's reply was, 'he had never been near enough to a parson to touch him with a barge pole, but if I must come, I might.' They soon became good friends and they were billeted together in the cellar underneath the village inn at Gris Pot.

The main part of the 69th Field Ambulance was located a few miles further back at a large brewery known as Fort Rompu which was situated on the banks of the River Lys approximately four miles from Armentières.[7] The basecamp was responsible for clearing the entire line. Generally speaking, all casualties were brought from regimental aid-posts by the Field Ambulance stretcher-bearers through communication trenches and then to the principal Advanced Dressing Stations (ADS) situated in the cellars of a house in Bois Grenier or the smaller ADS in the small hamlet of Gris Pot. Both were under direct observation from the dominating German held Aubers Ridge opposite, so the sick and wounded were evacuated by car, horse and motor ambulance after dark to the dressing-station located in the brewery, barn and outhouses of the farm at Fort Rompu.

5   TNA WO 95/2167/1.
6   Captain Philip Henry George Gosse (1879–1959). Grandson of naturalist Philip Henry Gosse (1810–88) and only son of poet, author and critic Sir Edmund William Gosse (1849–1928).
7   TNA WO 95/2179/1.

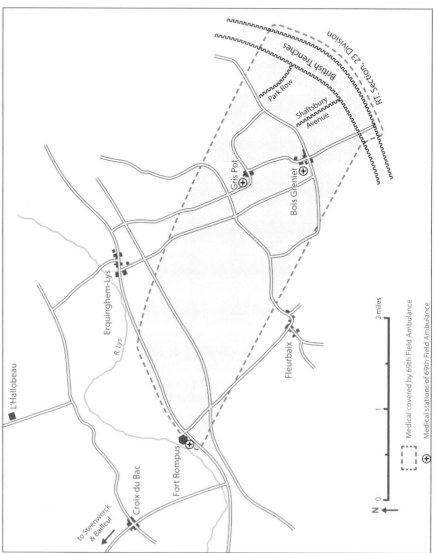

Map C Map showing area taken over by 69th Field Ambulance at the front on 14 September 1915. (George Anderson)

During the day, the villages and hamlets were deserted; after dark the scene would change as the whole area became alive with troops and transport, the roads became crowded with marching men, columns of ammunition waggons and horse-drawn ration carts. Vehicle lighting was forbidden; the drivers had to make the most of the flashes from flares and rifle fire, exploding shells, a little light from the trenches and if available, the moonlight, from a clear sky, in order to reach their destinations.

Herbert described his assigned village billet in a private post-war account:

> A mile behind the British front line trench, and parallel with the line, are two rows of cottages, this is the village of Gris Pot (pronounced by the initiated 'Gree Poe' but by the English fighting man, Grease Pot)! Five months ago scarcely a house was touched, though the fields around were scarred with shell holes. At the end of the row was a small inn: and here two doctors and myself met from our various duties and for all our meals.
>
> It was a tidy little room, looking away from the trenches, and into the cobbled road by which, when darkness came, troops and transports poured by on their way to the firing line. It looked also, through an archway in the opposite row – into the mouths of a row of Howitzer guns.

In October 1915, Herbert wrote again with his normal cheer:

> Beloved Little People,
> Here we are: here is our cellar: here is winter: here are the mice, the shells, a few roses, and many problems.
>
> I have a bowl of real live roses beside me: (though the 'bowl' is an old milk tin!) they are gathered from the shattered gardens hereabouts.
>
> These are my trench days: and they are full of many interesting details: some of which might edify you; some otherwise! Picture me today, in a dug-out occupied by the Battalion boot maker and his two assistants. Three privates, beside myself, sit there; all in bootless feet while the good man does our repairs while you wait and with no charges! In my case it is to have a set of jolly good hob nails driven into the soles of my boots, too slippery as they were for these trench board-walks. I have hopped on the boot maker by chance; and this bit of work gives me the chance of a chat and a smoke: and behold I rise having made half a dozen new friends.
>
> Tonight I have picked up a party of six men, – forming a guard, hopelessly lost! I took pity, and led them to their post. It was a three mile journey, or more: and I won't go into details of the locality, etc.; but when I left them I thought some of them were going to embrace me!
>
> So, one jogs along! I think after the experiences of the week, I have nearly found my 'war legs', not quite at some things, the perspiration will yet appear! But by next time I will be war-hardened, I hope!

It will take me some three or four months to begin to make myself felt: I'm a slow old cuss, with few ideas, and I'm hardly the man for the job. But one can only plod along and hope for some far off harvest from the woefully scant sowing.

Best of best love to you both, you very dear little people. God be praised for you.

In early October, the 13th DLI Battalion marched from the billets at Erquinghem-Lys to trench numbers 58 – 55, relieving the men of the 12th DLI Battalion.[8] The rain was heavy and the enemy unusually quiet for some time. At this point, the primary danger was the German sniper. Sadly these snipers, specially trained marksmen, were successful in picking off careless or unaware soldiers with devastating results causing men to be injured with head wounds which were often fatal.

After the war, Herbert described one of the first men he knew in his assigned battalion who was lost by such an incident with a German Sniper on the front line:

A few nights later I had a glimpse of his face as they trudged through the darkness and the rain to their first night in the trenches. And I little thought that he would be our first casualty. But a few nights later, duty took him out into No Man's Land. I know the way he went, for I went most of it myself a little later – and came back whole, thanks to a careless German Sniper! It looks a very long way from one of those farthest Listening Posts back to the shelter of one's own trenches: and the bit of broken soil ahead between oneself and the enemy parapet seems full of horrible possibilities. He was there, right against the enemy wire. And then – well the all too familiar story: a star-shell: a volley: … and his companion was more fortunate than he, and succeeded in bringing back the Sergeant's body.

There was something almost childlike about the peace of his face, lying there where a quiet sunlight kissed it on the morrow. And that together with the covetable witness of those who had known him, seemed to throw a very new force in the words I read over his open resting-place – 'He that believeth in me, though he were dead yet shall he live!'

It was a strange service. I wish you could see that little burial-place: an old village orchard, in whose trees the birds sang morning and evening as if by choice. There were a few flowers in the grass, and long trails of crimson creeper hung from the cottage walls on two sides. Even while the firing party took their places by the grave-side, two great shells came screaming into the adjoining garden, and burst with an angry crash. The men must lie down under the nearest wall: and even as I stood there reading the service, every British gun in the fields behind chose the time to talk back to the German gunners. Yet, for all the hellish din of the moments, the peace of that laying-by seemed unbroken: and when his

8   TNA WO 95/2182/1.

comrades had gathered from the shattered gardens around a handful of flowers, and placed them on the upturned soil; one felt that there was something triumphant about the passing of the Sergeant.

That is a very ordinary story: but I have told it for that very reason. For perhaps the sacrifice of the unnoticed man has won England's greatest glories.

The firing party described in Herbert's letter indicated that this was most probably an officer's burial, although despite his clear recollections, it is not possible to actually name the sergeant or officer encountered on that fateful day. However, the details related in his correspondence may be that relating to Lieutenant Philip Anthony Brown who was mortally wounded on the night of 4/5 November 1915. Brown's companion could well have been Private (later Lance Sergeant) Thomas Kenny who was the first DLI Victoria Cross recipient during the First World War. A month later, *The London Gazette* announced the citation stating his 'pluck, endurance and devotion to duty were beyond praise' whilst extracting Brown from No Man's Land under enemy fire. Also, it is interesting to note, the Senior Chaplain, the Rev. J. Nelson Blakiston, described Brown's burial in a private correspondence to Brown's mother:

> We laid the body to rest in a little military cemetery behind the lines on November 5th. Such a quiet and reverent service and several of his brother officers were there. At the close a small guard of honour gave a final salute to our fellow comrade. The spot is at a place called 'La Guernarie', about two or three miles south west of Armentières.

The use of the words, 'We laid', implies that the Rev. Blakison may not have been the only Army Chaplain conducting the service and thus possibly indicating further that the narrative written by the Rev. Cowl was for Lieutenant Philip Anthony Brown.[9]

No man wanted to be forgotten and left behind in the mud of Flanders. It was comforting for the soldiers to know and be re-assured that if the worst fate should come to them; the padre, a good man would inter them and send them to Heaven with the full blessing of God!

The 13th DLI war diarist recorded days of enemy bombardment hitting 'the front line of the division with high explosives, shrapnel and some whizz bangs'.[10] Shells often passed over the front line to strike support and reserve trenches, often disabling the support network. German and British aeroplanes were also operating in the area and often circled overhead. Some were occasionally brought down during aerial duels and anti-aircraft fire (which came from both sides). Herbert, acutely aware of

9   No death recorded for a sergeant in the 68th Brigade to match the location or date of this casualty.

10   TNA WO 95/2182/2.

the situation, wanted to experience with his men, the dangers of the bombardment and as their Army Chaplain he wanted to share the dangers and risks. He wrote the following:

> Even poor little I discarded a white dog-collar in the trenches when I found it attracted the attentions of German snipers: one young hopeful put five bullets round my head in as many seconds!

On at least one occasion, Herbert went 'over the top' with his men which, once again, would have created a great impression, especially as he did not have a gun in his possession!

By now it would have been clear that the trenches were like rabbit warrens from which they were to engage the enemy. Men had to learn to live and sleep in them for lengthy periods of time – five days in the front line; five in support and five in reserve – until the 23rd Division was relieved and placed in corps or army reserve.[11] However, the men had to make a home of these trenches so they would often make their little dug-outs into perfect little rooms and use them for cooking, reading and resting while others were on guard, alert and ready for imminent action!

During quiet periods, the 13th DLI improved the trench parados (an elevation of earth behind a fortified place as a protection against attack from the rear, especially a mound along the back of a trench).[12] There were some dull and foggy days at Erquingham-Lys during mid-October and in the 68th Brigade's war diary this period was recorded as being 'quiet and uneventful', despite the casualties.[13] It was during this time that Herbert travelled to nearby Armentières to see the latest screening of one of the newly released Charlie Chaplin films.[14] He later described the strange experience of viewing the film in the makeshift cinema, 'while shells crashed a hundred yards away'.

The 13th DLI and the 11th Northumberland Fusiliers would, as part of the normal trench routine, regularly relieve the 12th DLI and the 10th NF and vice versa. The ensuing activity must, in turn, have added some confusion in terms of Herbert knowing the location of his men. Two weeks later the trench numbers would change again which would not have helped his situation trying to keep in touch with the location of his men.[15]

On the 19th October, Herbert wrote to his parents. He was finally finding his way and establishing a presence throughout the 68th Brigade:

11   *Oldham Chronicle*, 2 October 1915.
12   TNA WO 95/2182/2.
13   TNA WO 95/2181/1.
14   Universally loved, Charlie Chaplin films were screened across France and Flanders to boost morale.
15   TNA WO 95/2182/3.

Mother Mine,

Muriel will probably have told you where I am and I hope you have a copy of the map I recommended to her – 'Daily Mail Bird's Eye Map of the British Front' Northern Section.

I expect to be in my cellar several weeks more, but never know for certain. When I come out, I hope it will be for a week's leave!

Things are very quiet with us at present, – so far as quietness goes in this part of the world. And best of all, the weekend has brought me the greatest encouragement in my work. I am beginning to find my feet and to get the measure of my opportunity, which is a great comfort to me. I don't mind anything so long as I can 'get busy' for the Great Master. Short of that, I'm miserable.

Could you have found me last night (Tuesday) you would have climbed the steps to a great rambling loft in an old deserted farm, just out of the fire-zone. In a broken chair you would have seen the padre seated, using all the wisdom Miss Pignell [Herbert's former school mistress] ever taught him! Round him on the floor were about 20 armed men, singing too for all they are worth. On two jutting beam ends are stuck three guttering candles – all the light we can muster, and we have covered the glass-less windows and gaps in the roof, lest any of this excessive radiance should attract the eye of a watchful German gunner. You would have heard the old favourite hymns as they have seldom been sung and would have felt the warming of those hearts as we prayed for you at home.

Breastwork trench, winter 1915-16. (Author's collection)

As I write they are marching by in the cold darkness to retake their places in the trenches.

Sunday was a great day: the best yet. Two stirring services in the morning: one in the same loft; the other in an old theatre three miles away. Then 10 miles back to my own Field Ambulance for evening service. I had notified both yeomanry and transport, so to my joy found the Dining Hall full with 200 men and a fine service.

Afterwards the C.O. called me aside and told me that, though he was a strict and life-long churchman, yet he had received more good through the last four Sunday evening services than ever in his life before; that he felt he 'dared not miss them'. He found a freedom and reality in them that was quite new to him. And so on. I was amazed, as I thought he only came to lend a courteous official recognition to them. So you see, I'm 'getting busy' at last!

The next day, 20th October, the 13th DLI was temporarily attached to the 24th Infantry Brigade (8th Division) and moved into support billets at Jesus Farm whilst handing over the trenches to the 12th DLI. Reliefs being a constant active service occurrence, one can appreciate how Herbert might lose temporary touch with his men during the frequent changeovers.

On Sunday 24th October there was a cold easterly wind as the battalions enjoyed the mandatory Church Parades along with a Roman Catholic Mass which was held at 7:30 a.m. at Jesus Farm. Sport, a popular diversion at the front, was represented by an afternoon football match, the 13th DLI defeating the 2nd Northampton Regiment; final score 2:1.[16]

In a post-war recollection, Herbert recalled Sunday memories at the front:

Amongst all the other duties, those were great days for preaching, if one felt there was a word relevant to these living, struggling, dying men. For my last few Sundays, services began at 9.00 am on Sunday, in the front line, and continued right through the support lines till they reached the Divisional Base, seven or eight miles behind. They were 10 in number. But the best of all was the last, in a school in the little town of Steenwerck. It held no more than 2 to 300: but the service built up till it was packed close and the big windows were few and men crowded in to them in the dark outside. One night the Colonel of my unit and all the officers available, were sitting there. One night as he left, I thanked him for his interest and support. When all the men had left, I found him waiting in the shadows. 'You were wrong to thank me. The fact is that I could not carry on without this service.'

16   TNA WO 95/2182/2.

The last week of October was relatively quiet with various working parties assigned to different sectors and base areas. Night patrols continued in the narrow muddy strip of No Man's Land which separated the German and British lines.

November arrived with very bad weather – more winter rain, high winds, cold temperatures and frequent fog.[17] On 3rd November, the 13th DLI's diarist observed: 'Wind fresh. North. Weather Wet. Trenches inundated parapets and dugouts caving in. Enemy quiet.'

Herbert writes home with little news from the front line, other than that of his cellar companions:

> Beloved Little Mother,
> Sorry to be so long writing this week, but it has been fairly busy or at least a lot of tramping about.
>
> News is nil just now. In fact letters are rather a problem.
>
> What do you think we dined from yesterday – pheasant, bred and born in the New Forest! Dr Gosse, who received the bird, has a practice in the New Forest and lives at Beaulieu! He is the son of Edmund Gosse, the author, ('Father and Son') and is a great character. He took the practice because it was a good centre for nature study. He buys up rare birds, keeps them in a big aviary in his garden long enough to learn their habits and then liberates them. Knows all the English birds, with all their haunts and manners. Next to birds, mice claim his first attention. Up here he spends hours over them. Yesterday, he walked to A----- [Armentières] and came back with pockets full of mouse-traps!! He sets them in the ditches round our Brewery and spends half the day skinning and setting these mice. He has caught one here that was almost unknown at the British Museum. Humans come third and last, I imagine, and are only studied in sufferance.
>
> He sleeps in the cellar with me, and is full of a very dry, quiet sort of humour that sometimes threatens to choke me entirely! He calls me 'Charlie', because I am a 'Chapl(a)in'!

One of Herbert's favourite past-times was bird-watching, and he would have been comforted at the presence of the skylark close to the front line. Its distinctive song flight was 'like the voice of God'. Singing high, rising and soaring in the skies over Flanders, it was, more often than not, the only bird that could be heard in the trenches, especially during brief moments of silence between the thunder and roaring of the heavy guns and the bursting of bombshells. Although there would be moments of quiet contemplation, there was always the imminent emphatic confirmation of the dangerous probabilities that surrounded the men at the front.

17   TNA WO 95/2182/4.

When back in the comparative comfort and relative safety of billets, Herbert would have enjoyed sharing his interest and knowledge of birds with his friend and fellow naturalist Dr Gosse.

Herbert outlined his duties in the Casualty Clearing Station (CCS) where he was based, although, from his next letter, it was clear that he believed his role was better carried out in the trenches rather than in the slightly safer environment of the CCS:

> They are only with us just long enough to be dressed, and are then sent straight down to the Casualty Clearing Station. There are always Chaplains attending to them. My duties are more with the men who are actually fighting, and I am attempting to establish a kind of ministry in the trenches. Practically all the other Chaplains work farther back: in our own brigade for instance, the R.C. is concerned exclusively with his own men at wayside confessionals, I believe. The C. of E. men keep out of the fire, gone as much as possible. One is at the Divisional Rest Camp. One has a club in the 'Resting Area' (I must explain all this when I come home: not permissible now.) I hold undisputed possession of the parish comprising our bit of the firing line.
>
> Now this is nothing like so risky a proceeding as you will possibly imagine. In fact, the trenches are wonderfully safe. You can hear the bullets flying overhead, but could not possibly be hit by them. Casualties occur either by foolhardiness, or during work in front of the trenches.
>
> Of course the difficulty is in 'making good' such work. And until I am better known it is very difficult, beyond the moral effect it has: – most of them are rather astonished to see a Parson wading through the mud right in amongst them! But it remains to be seen what I can really make of such a ministry.

Then the letter reverts to more practical matters concerning parcels from home: 'No one knows why it is, but they keep parcels an awful long time somewhere.' However, we know from an article printed in the Rev. J.H. Bateson's 'Weekly War Despatch' in *The Methodist Recorder* entitled 'The Comfort Department', that Herbert had received and greatly appreciated parcels from home: 'The Rev. H.B. Cowl, acknowledging some parcels of comforts, refers to their helpfulness in his work as a Chaplain at the front – 'A man's gift maketh room for him'. These packages, posted by the clergy and the parishioners, included Bibles, reading material, clothing, tinned delicacies, tobacco and other luxury items, were shared out by Herbert to his comrades. Indeed, in early November, *The Methodist Times*, in an article entitled, 'Lead the Soldiers to Christ' observed:

> Rev. H.B. Cowl, acknowledging some parcels received from the Packing Department, says that he finds the contents very useful in his trench visitation.
>
> I get into the trenches almost every day, especially when it is wet, as the men are then mostly in their dug-outs and unoccupied. Yesterday I saw a man coming off look-out duty for the machine-gun. It was blowing scuds of icy rain, and he

BOIS GRENIER

Pre-war picture of Bois Grenier village life. (Jack Thorpe)

was well soaked. He must crawl into the damp dug-out until his turn comes again. I saw him pull out his pipe and fill it, ransack his pockets for a last match, and ruefully put back his pipe. I assure you that I blessed the good-hearted Methodists who had sent me along just then with a pocketful of matchboxes. I am afraid the good people who attach addresses do not always get answers from the men; but it is not because their gifts are unappreciated – the men are glowingly grateful for every detail of these things, but the difficulties of writing in the trenches are very great. The days now are drab and quiet, so far as things can be quiet around here, but these are the days of a chaplain's opportunity. I wish I could urge all those who are working with the men in training at home this winter to do their utmost to lead them to Christ before they come away out here. The endless perils and hardships of these days are such that there seems little prospect of religious influences reaching many. Of course, we hope that as we settle down to the regular routine of winter quarters, we may be able to do more in this particular direction.[18]

With the heavy rain continuing unabated, Herbert wrote home to his mother, making new detailed requests for some practical trench attire:

18   *The Methodist Times*, 4 November 1915.

Would Father please enquire for me about something like waders? My trouble is that when it is raining hard the wet gets at my knees, between the top of my Gum Boots and the bottom of my Burberry.

The G.B.'s are grand for when it is not actually raining or raining much, but I want either something like cycling 'legs', or waders. Would you please ask sometime soon when he is in Brum [Birmingham] at some good Military Outfitters? I don't mind what I pay, in reason, as I feel the good pay we get ought to be used for thorough and proper equipment, first. If he would find out one or two different kinds of things that they suggest and let me know, with illustrations if possible, I will ask him to get them for me.

I'm afraid leave won't be as soon as I hoped: we may have to wait some weeks for our turn, but we don't know yet. I have the roughest post in the Division, so ought to get an early preference.

Dear old Mukie writes me such beautiful letters! I did not know she 'had it in her' so to speak! I am thankful for so grand a little sister!

We have a stove in our cellar now, which has done a lot to improve it – it is in the men's compartment, but airs the whole.

The two Doctor's servants cook our food, and do it quite well. The Doctors change every fortnight.

I think mittens and socks are the most acceptable things out here; also mufflers. Many folk make the 'mits' too small. They don't want to be huge, of course, but if too small they are useless. I will be very grateful for the things you good people promise. No one here seems to have ever heard anything of Red X stamps. They are like many other things described to you at home – conspicuous by absence! e.g: chicken: 'thousands sent per week to the men in the trenches', as the men say when they see it in the papers – "I don't think!"

Reading is rather a problem here. One can't carry books but I think I shall try Blackwoods Magazine, and send it on to Father when I have done with it.

Good-bye, Little Mother. I will try to write more intelligently next time.

On the morning of Tuesday 9 November 1915, Herbert's war in Flanders was about to come to an abrupt and painful end.

5

Wounded and Blighty Bound

At the beginning of November 1915, Herbert was billeted in the cellar of the Gris Pot village inn, half a mile behind the 69th Field Ambulance's ADS near Bois Grenier. The nights were cold and the mornings invariably frosty with mist. Occasional rainstorms inundated the area. Fighting was intermittent and winter had arrived. Herbert described his location and gave his parents an insight into his temporary living conditions:

> In the cellar of the shattered brewery where I lived for 8 weeks, the Doctors came and went week by week: for it was used as the Advanced Dressing Station and was not reckoned healthy for a stay of more than one week.
> Things were quiet there just then.

Daily life had become a combination of routine and terror:

> We messed at a little inn, a mile back from the trenches: and the road by which we passed to and fro was by no means a healthy place: punctuated with shell-craters, a goal for half-spent bullets from the German snipers; and without a shred of shelter beyond a blade of grass. This piece of road the Doctor would gladly have given half his pay to have escaped. But as duty led us that way two or three times each day, there was nothing for it, but to find some salve for jumpy nerves. This took the inglorious form of a mouth organ: and how often he and I plodded back to our cellar thro' the darkness to the enheartening strains of our one and only tune 'The Cock of the North'. Imagine the scene when at the onset of the journey a sentry's challenge was given, – "Halt! Who are you?" the music ceases abruptly, and from one or the other the reluctant confession is wrung – "Doctor and Chaplain!" The chuckle of the sentry was no matter of imagination!

During his last days at Gris Pot in Flanders, Herbert warmed to his new friend, Philip Gosse the doctor, for his qualities as a man of substance and those memories remained with Herbert for the rest of his life:

Large howitzer of the type near Gris Pot. (Author's collection)

I watched my Doctor the first time he came under heavy shell fire: and as I suspected, I have seldom seen a man so racked with manifest fear: I cannot imagine a man more unnerved. But it was at this very point that courage awoke and took over control of the man. The first man was hit, and he lay out there on the road where the shells were falling. In a moment my Doctor was out through the open window and bent low, was doubling down the road to his help. Twice we thought he must be hit: but nothing could turn him till he had reached and saved his man. And there we saw the real hero, the hero that is not always in those who are so called: the man who is first shaken by fear as a reed by the wind, and then goes to his deed of courage is the true hero.

It was Tuesday 9 November 1915 in Flanders. It was a wild and windy day and one that was to be particularly significant for Herbert:

I had returned that morning from some hours in the trenches (and out of them, at a Listening Post between the front line and the German trenches!); spread my mud-caked legs in front of a struggling little fire; and was on the point of devouring a very welcome tin of bully-beef, a long-drawn howling, slithering squeal announced the approach of a German shell. A heavy thump: a tearing crash – and then the very modest clatter of splintering glass and tumbling bricks which indicates the collapse of the back of the house. The mind works very quickly at such moments.

A shell announced the fact that the Bosches had brought up some heavy guns and were searching for an important battery just behind our Inn.

The first shell brought in the back of our house. The second lifted a cottage two doors away clean out of the row. We only waited for the third, which missed the room in which we were stood by inches.

We stood in the bar of the inn – a strange little group. The two doctors and myself; the French peasant and his wife who own the inn, and who have stayed to do business with the English troops and the old dog who has settled with them from a deserted village near-by. The woman watches windows and bottles and glasses dance to fragments: and the man stoops in angry terror beside her. There is a strange look of bewildering fright in the old dog's face, as though he knew he was in peril from which he could not escape.

We then cleared out the men, and removed to a safe distance, to watch the excellent practice of the German gunners.

'High Explosives' is a thing to be personified. It is a strange thing to feel oneself in the presence of some awful force which tears houses to shreds, rocks the ground, and will toss a human life to the winds like chaff – how puny a man is in its presence! There a man's pride goes by the board. You may feel only annoyed at it and quite superior (in time!) to a bullet which hums past your head. But this great hurtling, shrieking tearing invisible Thing – what is a man before it?

The 69th Field Ambulance diarist recorded the destruction of Gris Pot's Advanced Dressing Station that afternoon:

The bombardment which had begun at about 1.45 p.m., consisted entirely of big Howitzer shells. The first shell fell short but after that they mostly got direct hits on the cottages and in the street. Everyone, soldiers and civilians, got away up the road before the houses started to fall in.

Herbert continues his recollection and account of the following events that fateful afternoon:

So, we cleared our men from the houses and from some way down the road watched the great shells search to and fro for the hidden guns. The Doctor and I stood, ahead of the men, watching for any who might have been left in the doomed houses. A hundred yards away a shell threw a huge column of stone and soil into the air. I tried to answer the Doctor's exclamation that they were getting nearer, when I was aware of an intolerable pressure on my right jaw. I would step into that open door-way, to be out of the way of falling stones. But why, having done so, was I plunged head foremost onto a stone floor thick with mud and dabbled with red? For a moment I lay there gazing through the glass-less window. The sky was a hazy blue; and white, watery clouds were heralding more rain – that meant more mud: and the cellar in which we slept would be green with mist when we turned in tonight!

Then the Doctor came and knelt at my side: and I remember the disgust with which I realised, as he asked me to lie still, that I was kicking furiously. Outside a voice called – 'Bring a stretcher! The Chaplain's hit' and another – 'Well, I reckon he's done!'

Captain Phillip Gosse, the doctor wrote the account of the day's tragic events in the 69th Field Ambulance War Diary detailing exactly what happened:

Capt. COWL C.F. was wounded in the face and throat rather badly. While I was dressing him Lt WOODROW, accompanied by Dr GRIFFITHS ASC M.T. showing the greatest courage ran to the dressing station to try to get out the motor ambulance. This they found buried under debris. Lt WOODROW then tried to get into the house to get dressings for Capt. COWL but the doorway was blocked up with debris; as they turned to run back a high explosive fell, wounding Dr GRIFFITHS. Then another shell exploded and blew open a way into the dressing station. Lt WOODROW notwithstanding the great danger again returned, this time accompanied by a Sgt WALTER, RAMC, and got in the building by the way made by the last shell. Having got the required dressings, they began running back when a shell fell and burst apparently a few feet from them. Both were knocked down by the explosion and Lt WOODROW was wounded in the left arm. All these, Lt WOODROW, Sgt WALTER, and Dr GRIFFITHS all showed the greatest bravery as the shells were falling in the one place they had to cross. Dr GRIFFITHS was carried in by Pte CHURCH, whose conduct under fire I had reason to report to you four days ago. Sgt Phillip GOSSE, Lt WOODROW RAMC and Capt. COWL C.F. sent to CCS BAILLEUL: Dr GRIFFITHS ASC to special hospital, 26th Field Ambulance BAC ST MAUR.[1]

The 68th Brigade War Diarist noted:

Enemy shelled GRIS POT heavily, lifting Adv. Dressing Station 69th Field Ambulance severely wounding Rev. H.B. Cowl, and killing 1 S.B.[2] Other Casualties: 12 D.L.I. W[3] 1 OR.[4]

For his part, the 13th DLI diarist also reported that a Wesleyan chaplain had been wounded that afternoon, by the name of 'Cowell'.[5]

1   TNA WO 95/2179/1.
2   Stretcher Bearer.
3   Wounded.
4   Other Rank.
5   TNA WO 95/2182/2.

The Roman Catholic Army Chaplain, the Rev. Father Kean had developed a great fondness for his fellow padre and in a letter home to England, which was later published in the *Oldham Chronicle*, under the title 'Great Heroism', he wrote about what had happened to the young Wesleyan Army Chaplain:

> There was such an unfortunate thing happened to a young Wesleyan chaplain a short time ago. We were both billeted in close proximity to the firing line. One day the Germans started shelling and drove my friend and the medical officers out of their quarters. Mine remained intact. I invited them all to come into my billet for a time. They had hardly entered when a shell caught the first dressing station, and blew it sky high. After a short interval the chaplain and a medical officer left my room, and hardly had they crossed the threshold when the poor chaplain was shot [hit by shrapnel]. He fell bleeding most profusely. We all ran out to assist him, and a call was made for the ambulance. But the poor fellow who ran for it was shot [hit by shrapnel] likewise. While I was bending over the fallen chaplain with a medical officer attending him, another doctor and orderly ran for dressing, when another shell came and exploded close to us and wounded them, but I escaped. We had to carry all the wounded to a dug-out in the open field made for the use of the artillery. One died, and the others were seriously wounded. The poor chaplain's woes were not yet finished.

Father Kean continued to write about what happened next to Herbert:

> He was so brave, kind and dauntless. When we carried him streaming with blood to the dug-out he would not have us place him in it until we had first comfortably arranged the fallen soldiers, and on entering he clasped the hand of his wounded companion. A cry was made for water. This was brought with all haste, and when we offered it to the dying private, he refused to drink before it had been given to the chaplain. 'Let the parson have it first,' said the dying private. This was real heroism.
>
>   These were the last words spoken by the private.[6]

Herbert had no idea of the background events that took place on that day to save his life. He did not know then the details that have emerged with the release of War Diaries in more recent years. He would not have known that a man by the name of Alfred Griffiths would die the following day as a result of wounds sustained in attempting to save his life – the life of the injured Chaplain. After a short stay in hospital, Lt Woodrow who sustained a broken arm was soon able to return to active service.[7]

---

6   *Oldham Chronicle*, 9 December 1915.
7   TNA WO 95/2179/1.

Gosse concluded the entry in the Field Ambulance Diary that day with a note reporting the 'bravery of Lt WOODROW, Sgt WALTER, Dr GRIFFITHS and Pte CHURCH on 9 November 1915.'

Herbert subsequently reflected on the initial moments when he was struggling for life:

> Small white clouds drifted across the autumn sky and his anxious head [Gosse] seemed part of that ultimate peace. When the shelling lifted, and my stretcher was pushed into an ambulance, the R.C. Padre climbed in and stood beside me to keep me from choking on the five mile journey to a Field Hospital.

Herbert recalls his very last memories of Flanders:

> My last glimpse of that place will always be clear to me. I lay on the stretcher in the motor ambulance which had been hurried up, all around it stood those men with whom I had lived for weeks. And, as I looked into that crowd of faces and waved them good-bye, and tried to speak my Master's name, how I longed for voice enough to speak just then for Him!

One of his strongest recollections of that day which stayed with him (and almost haunted him) for many years, was the image of the men from his battalion, who had rushed back from the trenches to see him. They were standing and kneeling beside him and his inability to speak to them upset him greatly. Herbert had survived his initial injuries and with no blood transfussions at the front line, with such loss of blood, his survival could have been considered the first miracle of his story as an Army Chaplain.

From 25th August to 7th November 1915, the 23rd Division War diarist recorded 360 men of the Durham Light Infantry had been killed in action. No figures for the total number of divisional casualties. The entry makes no mention of Army Chaplains.

In a semi-conscious state, Herbert, accompanied by the Roman Catholic chaplain (most likely to have been the Rev. Farther Kean) travelled by motor ambulance along a rough, shell-pitted track, as they headed back to the nearest Casualty Clearing Station (CCS) at Bailleul. Catholic chaplains had been advised in a booklet entitled, *Information and Hints*, to be on friendly terms with chaplains from other denominations but not to discuss religion with them. It is not known what was said to Herbert on that journey to the Casualty Clearing Station with the Roman Catholic padre. Later Herbert recalled:

> Consciousness never left me: For four or six hours after that there followed the grim struggle for life, and the wonder at each breath how the next could possibly come. A piece of shell – that proved afterwards to be as large as a thumb – had smashed through the jaw, through the roots of the tongue, and landed across the back of the throat.

Bailleul school building utilised by 8th Casualty Clearing Station. (Author's collection)

When Herbert arrived at Bailleul the priority would have been to halt bleeding from the wound. The medical staff could see that he was weak as a result of his wounds and that he was in a great deal of pain. He had lost a good amount of blood. At this point it was unclear if he would survive his injuries. One of the medical staff told Herbert that he was going to get brandy for him. Herbert was unable to speak and too weak to reject the offer. When he was younger he had visited poor communities and seen so much deprivation as a result of alcohol abuse that it had consolidated his views on the evils of drink. However, before he knew it, brandy was being poured into his mouth. He was about to get his first taste of liquor, but to everyone's astonishment the brandy simply gushed out from the side of his neck through the gaping hole. So, he kept to his beliefs and he never tasted the alcohol!

Some days passed before his condition stabilised and the doctors were ready to operate. The No.8 CCS War Diary records '136 admissions – 3 lying' – one of whom was Herbert.[8]

Remarkably and in true form, the next day Herbert found the strength to pencil a letter to his father. Whether he was under the influence of morphine or not is uncertain, but the cheerful content is quite incredible given the circumstances. The letter to his father, which was actually mistakenly dated November 9th (the day before) gives no account of Herbert's true situation, that he had been severely wounded and was

8   TNA WO 95/342/1.

in hospital waiting to be operated on as soon as it was safe to do so. This is his letter home:

> Beloved Little Super,
> This note is for you only – none of your reading it Mrs Cowl!
>   In her last letter the little mother described herself most beautifully in her cosy and cheery bed. Well, I guess I'm quite with her now. I too have got a gorgeous little shake down, and am feeling quite a prince, in the Casualty Clearing Station.
>   This does not mean that I have changed job, but that I am taking a little rest.
>   The rotten old Bosches blew our Dressing Station to bits yesterday; you should have seen the show! Incidentally, they dropped bits of steel on the doctor, 2 men and your worthy son!
>   I was very slightly hit – in a most unseemly place for a parson – the jaw! They carried me into a dug-out, and then by ambulance to head-quarters. Just as we were swinging off to the Casualty Clearing Station at B xxx [Bailleul], I heard a voice saying, 'is that you Herbert?' Who should it be but dear old Bob Harding! [a second cousin] Heaven bless him! He has been in here again this morning to see me!
>   Well, the X-Ray man performs on me this afternoon – then for a jolly good holiday – pip – pip!! Good old 'Blighty'!
>   So, see you soon, all being well. Best love to 'ye both'

At this point the doctors had to decide how best to treat the Padre's injuries. The practice was to get wounded soldiers fixed quickly and returned to the battle front for action. The seriously wounded were transported back to a Base Hospital before being taken back to Blighty by hospital ship and on to a suitable hospital in England for further treatment. In Herbert's case, the next step for the doctors at the 8th Casualty Clearing Station was to devise an instrument to remove the precariously positioned shrapnel from his throat.

Eventually, the jagged piece of iron was successfully removed.

Herbert was so unwell that he remained at the CCS for a few more days until the doctors decided he was stable enough for transfer to a Base Hospital in Boulogne and then to be returned home to England.

On reflection, he later observed:

> … and for weeks from that moment, my only way of travelling about the world was on a stretcher!
>   I had three days at the Casualty Clearing Station, being unfit to be moved: and got only about an hour's morphia-sleep a night, and no food or drink (save blood) of any sort. Then they took out of my throat the shell casing …'

Something Herbert later described as being 'a hair's breadth from the jugular'.

The next letter home is sent from Bailleul to Herbert's father on November 15th, following the successful operation to remove the shrapnel from his neck:

> Beloved Little Super,
>
> You see I am still lolling about at this C.C.S. Fact is, they have taken rather a fancy to me. I am the doctor's pet case – he is as fond as punch of his operation on me! Also, the nurses and orderlies call me the "best yet" since they opened this officer's ward 9 months ago!
>
> Anyway, I'm doing fine. They move me today if the weather is fit; but I fear it won't be. When they do, I can't say – nor any one – how long it will be before they move me on again to England. Probably only a few days. I will let you know directly I can. I can't request for any particular place from this side; but I may be able to get transferred when I get to England. I should ask to go to Bath, I think, wouldn't you?
>
> That's all I can do now. Best love to both.
>
> Cheer up _____

Herbert never wrote a detailed account of the actual journey from the CCS to the Base Hospital, apart from stating it was 'an awful twelve hours by Hospital Train from B xxx [Bailleul] to Boulogne'. However, he does mention the tedious journey in a letter sent to his parents on the last Sunday that he was in France:

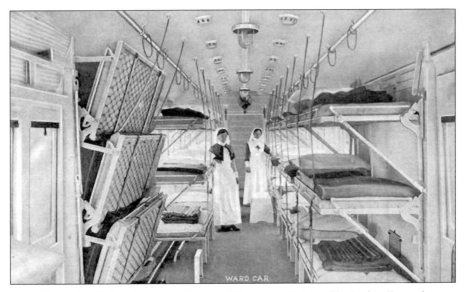

Hospital train interior; the reality was different for Herbert. (Author's collection)

Beloved Little People,

This is nearly Father's Service time, I expect; and I am not forgetting him. I expect I shall be in England this time next week, tho' what part I have no idea. They say three or four days here. I have a lovely little bedroom (shared with a Canadian) which looks straight out to sea, down the Channel. Lovely room. Good companion (if only I could talk to him!). Doctors all pleased with me. Nurses all wonderful. Yesterday's Red Cross train journey (12 hours) – well, I'll spare your feelings!

More anon.

A telling little postscript added the heartening news: 'P.S. (Later) 2 hrs sleep this afternoon! Hooray! Best yet.'

He had been taken to Hotel Christol which was in fact No.7 British Red Cross Hospital – the 'Allied Forces Base Hospital' located on the quay by the harbour in Boulogne. Before the war it was a well-known and established four-storey 19th century hotel used by travellers passing through the town. It was located near the port on the north bank of the Liane River and had been rapidly commandeered by the military in 1914. Now it was converted into a hospital with 189 beds. Motor Ambulances were parked outside the hotel on the quay, in readiness for transporting the wounded. Hotel Christol with its 145 Red Cross staff, was one of 17 hospitals designated to care for the wounded in and around the town. There were 10 regular and 7 voluntary hospitals all under military control. Many local large houses and hotels were also used as convalescent hospitals.

My room in Hospital with a few flowers, and much sunshine, looked out over the French cliffs, across the Harbour, and away down the English Channel. On Tuesday afternoon, to my great joy, my brother Methodist, Wesleyan Chaplain, Cecil Weeks visited me. As he was leaving, I asked him to read and pray. He turned; accidentally it seemed, to the 139th Psalm. I did not understand at the time why it was that the familiar verses came with such tremendous significance, and that the presence of God so filled the room as he read, 'Thou searchest out my path and my lying down ... If I dwell, in the uttermost parts of the sea, even there shall thy hand lead me, and thy right hand shall hold me.'

Writing home on his last day in Base Hospital, Herbert related his improved condition:

Dearest Motherkins,

Your parcel (with stockings, cake, biscuits, etc.) came the day before I took to picking up German scrap-iron. Indeed, I was just sitting down to lunch, from your tuck mostly, when a 'glorious detonation' fetched every bit of glass out of the house. Now I grieve to say all your good things are mingled in the dust of the fallen house!

Postcard showing Hotel Christol and the quay at Boulogne. (Author's collection)

I am getting on splendidly tho' of course it is, and it will be, a long job.

I wish I could hear from you, but it is not possible 'till I get settled somewhere. Can't manage more. Sorry! Best love!

Fond memories of Herbert's hospital experience were recorded following his return to England:

On arrival at Boulogne there began what might be called the 'explosion of luxury'. For in Boulogne I had a gorgeous little bedroom, flooded with sunshine, which was only second to the joy of seeing the refreshing faces of English women again. Sammy [Herbert's fond nickname for a Tommy], my boy! That's the place for you! Go and get pipped and then spend a few days in a Base Hospital; and I'll guarantee it cures you of your benighted misanthropisms!

In England, *The Methodist Recorder* printed the following article entitled, 'The Rev. H.B. Cowl Wounded':

Information has been received that the Rev. H.B. Cowl, C.F., was severely wounded at the Front on Nov. 9. The Rev. W. Meadowcroft, who has seen Mr. Cowl since the piece of shell that struck him was extracted from his neck, reports that the operation was entirely successful. The wounded Chaplain is getting on well, and is very cheerful. One of the soldiers under Mr Cowl's pastoral care has written to express, for himself and comrades, appreciation of Mr Cowl's services. 'He was always going backward and forward from billet to trench and trench to billet. He was just behind the trenches when he was hit. I shall never forget the last service we had with him in an old barn. We had missed the Sunday Church parade on account of the opportunity for a very much-needed bath. Mr Cowl arranged for us to have a service on the evening of the following day. It was a wretched night, and only six of us turned up, but 'where two or three are gathered together in My name, there am I in the midst of them,' was truly realised. We had a glorious time, a real Methodist Class-meeting. I can't say too much about the good work Mr Cowl was doing. 'How we shall miss him!' We hope that Mr Cowl will soon recover from his wounds and be able to continue the work which has been so helpful to the soldiers under his care.[9]

Meanwhile, Herbert's cellar mate, the doctor, Captain Phillip Gosse wrote to Herbert's father from Flanders:

Dear Mr Cowl,
I was with your boy when he was wounded. I hear that he is doing very well, has had the piece of shell removed and has gone to one of the hospitals at Boulogne: where hence he found a friend, just Woodrow, waiting for him. He had a lucky escape from worse things. I am looking after his parcels and will do as you wish and hand them on to Mr Meadowcroft.[10] I hear that your son was quite comfortable after they took out the bit of shell. He will be badly missed by his men who seemed to admire him: as he was not only their chaplain but also their friend, and spent hours with them in the trenches, instead of living in safety and comfort further back. I had some 10 days with him in a brewery cellar where we were both studying to play on the mouth organ.
    Please give him my love when you see him which will be pretty soon I expect.
    Yours Sincerely,
    Phillip Gosse
    Please ask him to drop me a line if he has time to write. PG

On the 17th November, Herbert was passed as fit and ready for the journey home. As he headed back to England, little did he realise that he would again experience another dramatic dice with death amidst a contemptible act of war. And so as his thoughts turned towards home and the thought of seeing loved ones, he embarked on another adventure which again was going to turn out to be another fateful day in his life!

9   *The Methodist Recorder*, 18 November 1915.
10 Ibid.

6

Crossing the Channel

It was Tuesday morning, 17 November 1915 and HMHS (His Majesty's Hospital Ship) *Anglia* was docked in the port of Boulogne, France, making her final preparations to transport the wounded and sick back home to England.[1] *Anglia* was a passenger steam ship built in 1900 for the London and North Western Railway. After being requisitioned by the military authorities in April 1915, she was refitted and painted in the livery colours of the Red Cross, turning her into a fully functional hospital ship to transport the wounded soldiers from France and Flanders home to England. She was originally fitted to carry 275 lying down cases, 31 being swinging cots, although in her first two months of operational service this number was reduced with alterations on-going to improve the practicalities of handling large numbers of injured soldiers.[2] With large red crosses clearly visible on her white-painted hull, HMHS *Anglia* was instantly recognisable as a non-fighting ship as per the Geneva Convention. Major J.M. Maynard Crawford RAMC, assisted by Captain W.J. Gow and Lieutenant P.L.T. Bennett with 28 RAMC NCOs,[3] was the OC[4] on board.[5] Three nursing staff were led by the Matron, Mrs Mitchell of the Queen Alexandra's Imperial Military Nursing Staff (QAIMNS).[6] By the late autumn of 1915, cross-channel hospital ships, including the *Anglia* would have been kept very busy with transporting many of the 60,000 casualties from the Battle of Loos being returned home to England.

Initially, on the morning of the 17th November, it was uncertain as to whether the *Anglia* would sail as the sea had been rough the night before and there was some concern that German mines may have broken loose from their positions in the Channel and pose a threat to nearby shipping.

However, Herbert was oblivious to this risk:

1   TNA ADM 1/8443/367.
2   TNA WO 95/4142/1.
3   Non-Commissioned Officers.
4   Officer Commanding.
5   TNA WO 95/4142/1.
6   Ibid.

> It was a happy morning when the Doctors informed me that they thought me
> out of danger, fit to be moved to England. The ground was white with snow and
> a cold sunshine made the last scenes of France quite gay. The 'Anglia' was a fine
> boat, and had a full load – about 400 in all, including just 13 officers!

At around nine o'clock he was taken down to the harbour and transferred by stretcher
to the hospital ship. On average two stretcher cases were carried up the gangway every
minute (depending on the severity of the individual cases), so loading would have
taken a number of hours throughout the radiant but bitterly cold morning.[7]

Herbert recalled:

> It was good to exchange a narrow stretcher for a cosy cot in the beautiful Officers'
> Saloon.

He was placed in the thirteenth bed in the Officers' Saloon. Once the injured and sick
soldiers were safely on board, HMHS *Anglia* was ready to leave France with a full load
of approximately 400 injured and wounded servicemen (166 were serious 'cot-cases',
meaning men gravely crippled and disabled), together with the ship's crew and the
complement of doctors and nurses to tend to the sick and wounded. At approximately
11:00 a.m. local time, a little later than planned, the ship pulled away from the quayside. As they left Boulogne, the weather was fine and clear.[8]

There was a slight northerly wind but the sea was smooth. The *Anglia* was capable
of a comfortable speed of 20 knots through the water and she headed for Dover taking
the route reserved solely for the hospital ships and which was marked by special
buoys. It would not have taken long from Boulogne for the Dover Cliffs to appear on
the horizon. The wind was increasing that day and the sea was beginning to swell.
However, the white cliffs of Dover would now be looming into sight as a safe reminder
of home:

> Four miles from Dover the Sister in charge was standing by my cot, arranging
> for new bandages to be put on. All round was comfort and order and seeming
> security.

At approximately 12:35 p.m. whilst the Queen Alexandra's Imperial Military Nursing
Service (QAIMNS) Sister and orderly were attending to Herbert, disaster struck the
Hospital Ship:

> I lay in a bed at the lower end of the Officers' Saloon. The Sister had just been
> speaking to me, when we were within less than four miles of Dover. It was a

7   Ibid.
8   TNA ADM 1/8443/367.

remarkable instantaneous thing: for in a second, – a second full of a stunning flash and a hollow roar – that palace of comfort and order was transformed into a pandemonium.

Herbert, like so many of the other men, addressed the nurse attending to him as Sister and whose identity his granddaughter was to uncover a 100 years later:

> The Sister stood beside my bed to explain there was too much movement, motion to attempt a dressing, when a searing flash filled the saloon, tore away the upper part of her head, doubled the orderly a few yards away like a broken stick and brought the sea surging across the floor.

The Sister was actually Nurse Mary Rodwell of the QAIMNS.

> The smiling face of the Sister was running blood: the orderly a few paces away was a lifeless heap against the wall: furniture, beds and fittings were a tumbling mass of wreckage.
>
> My iron cot was crumpled into scrap-iron, and I was tumbled into the water that raced in through the great gap in the bows. Opposite was a doorway and a long passage: and into this I was carried. Wreckage of all kinds was heaped on me and was crushing the breath from me, while the water completely covered me.

The huge explosion on board, as a mine collided with the *Anglia*, blew the bridge to smithereens and hurled waterspouts mountains high. An S.O.S. signal should have been sent, but the machinery for doing so had been destroyed.

It emerged that HMHS *Anglia* had been in the vicinity of No. 8 Buoy which was located four miles off the western entrance of Dover harbour. The Germans had laid mines in the sea and despite the best efforts of the Royal Navy minesweepers and vessels surveying and clearing the Channel, some mines remained undetected. HMHS *Anglia* had struck one of the mines laid by the minelayer German submarine U-boat, UC-5.[9]

In a subsequent report of the disaster, the order to stop the engines was given but the telegraph was damaged and the signal never reached the engine room so the engines continued to work and the ship kept moving even as it was beginning to list. The head of the ship then began to dip and the propellers were soon out of the water but still turning.[10] Herbert continues to describe the events unfolding below the deck in the officers' saloon:

9   Operating from naval bases on the Flanders coast, the UC type coastal submarines were a class of small minelaying craft built during the early part of the First World War.
10   TNA ADM 1/8443/367.

Crushed thus, choking with salt water, and stunned by the new wound in the head, I was carried some 20 feet down the passage. It was then that as I like to think, the Angel of God became my deliverer. For I found myself suddenly and unaccountably standing on my feet in the midst of the water and the wreckage. A few hours before I could not walk: but now I walked along the passage: only to find myself in a bathroom from which there was no escape.

It seemed now that there was no other way than to wait for the slowly rising water to fill the room.

By this time, other vessels in the area had spotted HMHS *Anglia* in trouble. Several vessels including the destroyers HMS *Hazard* and HMS *Ure*, in addition to other nearby craft, changed course to facilitate the rescue of passengers and crew. A passing London collier on her way to Lisbon, the lesser known SS *Lusitania*, also changed course and, in doing so, struck another drifting mine. There were 56 crewmen on board. Some reports stated all were rescued, but others noted 31 saved. The ship perished.

Etching depicting the sinking of HMHS *Anglia*. (Author's collection)

A scene of chaos and cruel confusion must have ensued as HMHS *Anglia* began to circle. The siren was jammed on.[11] One of her propellers was clear of the water and the other still submerged and this turned the doomed vessel to starboard, making it most hazardous and very dangerous for any of the rescue boats to come alongside

11   *Gun Fire*, Issue 57 (no date).

to transfer the men from the stricken ship. With the engines still working, the ship passed through the water at a rate which increased the speed with which she began to sink. At one point it was reported that, despite the steep angle of the deck, with the ship almost standing on her bows, a large number of men were able to jump to safety when one of the rescue boats bravely passed under the stern of the *Anglia* with the ship's propellers still spinning and racing around in mid-air. One wounded soldier from West Wickham in Kent, on board, described it afterwards as a situation of 'simply everyone for himself'.[12]

The Coxswain of H.M. *Torpedo* Boat No. 4, attached to the Dover patrol that fateful day, E. Crissup wrote a letter to the *Yorkshire Evening Post* after the sinking of the *Anglia*:

> When the torpedoed boat got alongside, it was difficult to make our orders understood, for a strange reason. The Anglia's siren was blowing the whole time. In the confusion that followed the explosion the siren cord had been pulled too hard, so that it jammed. To make matters worse, we dare not pass our wires or hawsers to secure the torpedo boat to the sinking ship because she would have dragged us to the bottom. We therefore did the best we could in the circumstances.
>
> In the meantime we had sent an S.O.S. to Dover for doctors and nurses to be ready to receive the wounded.[13]

The matron and her nursing sisters worked tirelessly to tie as many lifebelts on to the wounded and to evacuate the ship. As one survivor subsequently recounted:

> Faces white as death, you know; hair blowing loose in a bitter gale, and their hands and aprons smeared with blood from the dressing stations. No, I shall never forget! 'Fighting men first!' was the word our heroines passed.

The able-bodied but wounded soldiers had a better chance of escaping from the floundering *Anglia*; onto a gunboat, lifeboat, raft, or floating debris, but the fate of the seriously wounded, the 'cot-cases' was, more often than not, hopeless. Herbert was one of the lucky ones.

Herbert continued his personal fight to escape:

> Sitting on the bath side, I watched the water rising inch by quick inch. Then in an opposite mirror I saw a ghastly sight, which proved on reflection to be my own face – half covered with blood, the other – the other with the broken jaw hanging pretty loose! – a dirty grimmish white!

---

12 Ibid.
13 Ibid.

No man chooses to drown in a hole; so there began the grim struggle to climb the clogged passage and to gain the deck.

Fifteen minutes after the initial explosion, the steamship SS *Channel Queen* departed from Dover for Jersey. Steaming at approximately 10 knots, the *Anglia* was observed in difficulty. Proceeding for a quarter of a mile before halting, lifeboats were dispatched to rescue survivors before transfer to a nearby gunboat. In the meantime, Herbert had made his way to the main deck. The struggle continued:

> A boat was being launched crowded with men. It nearly reached the water, but the bow rope became entangled, and the whole boat full was thrown into the sea.
>
> Men on the deck were rushing wildly to and fro and no one seemed to care for the plight of those in the water. But on the back of the deck were a number of raft-seats. I found a gangway opening in the deck-rail, got it open, and managed to drag three or four rafts across the deck and drop them in among the drowning fellows beneath. I don't know if any got onto them and were saved: but the wonder to me was that when I came onto the boat, I was practically unable to stand: now I was running about the deck and doing a strong man's work!
>
> Once a torpedo boat ran along-side, but while a married man and I tussled for which should not go first, she was full and away again.
>
> But at last the end drew near: the deck tilted till a foothold was impossible; and climbing the rail, I sat on the side of the ship and waited the last plunge. Only a few men were left with me then – like so many on that boat, scared and cringing creatures.
>
> Then came the rush of the last wave, and the dark swirling waters closed over-head. But a good life-belt, and a few strokes, brought me to the surface again; and a short swim to a small raft.

HMHS *Anglia* sank at 1:20 p.m. Official maritime records note that she remained afloat for 45 minutes from the first explosion to sinking.[14] However, many if not most first-hand accounts indicate that the ship actually sank much faster, many eyewitnesses stating that it was more like twenty minutes or less.[15] The *Aberdeen Evening Express* described how: 'the *Anglia* seemed for one brief second to stand on her bows, and then disappeared.'[16]

> The last comes as usual, suddenly. A white foaming wave is rushing over the malaise: it closes in above, and one is in a swirling mass of dark waters.

14   TNA ADM 1/8443/367.
15   *Dover Express*, 26 November 1915.
16   *Aberdeen Evening Express*, 18 November 1915.

Herbert described the twenty minutes or so of floating in the cold, oil-covered water and of riding waves driven by a frigid north-east wind. His ultimate act of selflessness was to assist a fellow officer whom he believed needed his lifebelt more than himself! Herbert never wanted to be associated with, as he put it, 'ridiculous tales of "heroism"', but this is not how others saw his action on that eventful day.

> Coming again to the surface, I swam to a small safety-raft, and managed to pull myself up so as to lie across it. Yonder were the tall white cliffs of Dover, and in the foreground several feet of the masts of the Hospital Ship were still visible, with the Red Cross flag flapping briskly in the cold wind.
> Two men were near me in the water, and it was a small motor patrol boat that gathered us in, and hurried us into Dover at a record speed.

Herbert had an incredible knack of seeing the good in everything; his humour shone through even in the darkest of times:

> Had not kindly hands brought welcome blankets, my first appearance in Dover would have been more sensational than ecclesiastical: for by then my clothing amounted to a small wrist watch: which is now my only souvenir of active service!

Rescued from choppy waters by a passing patrol boat, he had finally arrived home in England. From the patrol boat he was wrapped in a warm blanket, lifted on to a stretcher and taken to Dover Station where he was put on a comfortable hospital train – destination London:

> A doctor from the quayside called – 'Where's this Army Chaplain? What you a Chaplain? Well, get onto my back: The Lord has been good to you this time, my boy!'

Herbert's only souvenir from active service. A very distinctive watch made in Switzerland with a silver casing and a gold plated winder which was, unusually, on the left side position indicating that he or somebody else had the time-piece possibly custom-made. A thin gold edging around the watch face no longer exists. (Author's collection)

Herbert, who never considered himself a hero, would not forget what he later determined as God's role during a deadly day culminating in improbable survival. The long train journey to London was later described as 'a fine altar' on which he was able to 'renew the ultimate sacrifice':

> That is all that I must tell now, save to add that I recognise the love of God in it all. It is easy to believe that it was God who brought me through that valley of the shadow of death: and because I believe that, I do not hesitate to believe that God sent me into it.

Approximately 134 men (including Irish and Canadian soldiers[17]) and one woman lost their lives in the *Anglia* disaster, despite the almost immediate assistance of nearby vessels. *The Times*[18] *Dover Express*,[19] among other newspapers reported that four officers, one nurse and 129 men were listed as missing and, on 22 January 1916, another man's name was added to the list of fatalities. There is still some conjecture about the number who died that day, but whatever the final and accurate number was in total, it does not detract from the tragedy. Nevertheless, *The Times*[20] reported: 'It was exceedingly fortunate that the disaster did not occur at night, or the death-roll must have been far greater.' Also, the sinking of the *Anglia*, a well-known vessel since conveying the injured King George V back from France[21] on the 31st October[22] was the first occasion when a hospital ship carrying wounded was sunk as a result of enemy action.

The mortal remains of 159 souls, including that of Nursing Sister Mary Rodwell, who perished whilst on HMHS *Anglia* lie undisturbed, the wreck site is one of the first of twenty-one war graves officially designated by the 1986 Protection of Military Remains Act. Today she lies undisturbed in 30 metres of water on a sandy seabed in the English Channel – the dead and their ship now rest in peace.

Herbert had not realised the full extent of personal injuries sustained during the initial explosion on the *Anglia*. He had been struck on the back of the head with such force that, in addition to his other injuries, there was a very deep gaping wound from ear to ear above the top back line of his neck. On arrival in London, he was immediately rushed to Beckett Hospital at 34 Grosvenor Street.

At the end of December 1914 the Hon. Mrs Beckett, wife of the banker, Major the Hon. Rupert Evelyn Beckett, opened the auxiliary hospital for officers. The Beckett Hospital, Grosvenor Street, near Hanover Square had 25 beds and was affiliated with the Queen Alexandra's Military Hospital at Millbank in London.

---

17   *The Toronto World*, 23-25 November 1915.
18   *The Times*, 29 November 1915.
19   *Dover Express*, 6 December 1915.
20   *The Times*, 19 November 1915.
21   The King was thrown of his horse whilst inspecting troops at Hesdigneul near Boulogne on 28 October 1915.
22   Gun Fire, Issue 57 (no date).

Two days after his arrival, a post office telegraph (telegram) was sent from the Secretary of the War Office to Rev. F.B. Cowl at 4:32 p.m. Addressed to Hampreston Manor Farm, Wimborne, Dorset (the home of Herbert's sister 'Mukie') informing him that his son had been wounded and was now 'admitted to 34 Grosvenor Street Hospital suffering from a wound to the head'.

The news of the *Anglia* disaster was announced in the British press, the grave headlines spreading across Europe and the world. *Le Gaulois*'s front page described 'Une Catastrophe' [a catastrophe] and 'les dernieres moments de vaisseau' [the ship's last moments].[23] *Le Figaro* and *Le Matin* followed suit.[24] Belgian papers, *L'echo de la Presse*[25] and *Le Bien Publique*,[26] repeated the story as issued to them by the Reuters news agency. The *New York Times* reported the disaster on 18th November with the headline:

BRITISH HOSPITAL SHIP SUNK, 85 LOST; The *Anglia*, with 300 Wounded Aboard, Hits a Mine in the Channel. COLLIER ALSO GOES DOWN. She Was Another Lusitania – Many Hospital Ship Victims Drowned in Bed.

The Methodist Recorder noted Herbert's survival:

The Rev. H.B. Cowl Saved from the Hospital Ship 'Anglia.'

The Rev. H.B. Cowl, who was severely wounded at the Front a few days ago, was on board the Hospital Ship 'Anglia,' en route for home, when it was sunk by an enemy mine about three miles out of Dover. Mr Cowl had a thrilling experience, but happily escaped with his life. Immediately the 'Anglia' struck the mine which sent her to her doom, the water rushed in to the saloon, where a number of wounded officers lay, through the hole which the explosion made in the ship's side.

The article went on to describe the events of that terrible time and Herbert's recognised role in saving as many men as possible:

Fortunately, Mr Cowl had been able to put on a lifebelt, and, though drawn far down by the sinking ship, quickly rose to the surface of the sea. After swimming for some time he found a raft, to which he clung until a naval vessel came to his assistance, and kind hands took him on board. Despite his severe wounds, received behind the trenches, further wounds received on the ship and in the sea in his struggle for life, shock and exhaustion, Mr. Cowl is doing well. He is at

23   *Le Gaulois*, 19 November 1915.
24   *Le Figaro* & *Le Matin*, 18 November 1915.
25   *L'echo de la Presse*, 19 November 1915.
26   *Le Bien Publique*, 23 November 1915.

present lying in a London Hospital, receiving every possible attention, thankful that his life has been spared for further service, and buoyed up with hope of a speedy and complete recovery. Many tributes to the work and influence of Mr Cowl have been received.

The *Birmingham Gazette* also reported on Herbert's courage in a newspaper article detailing his heroic actions, throwing rafts to soldiers who were drowning in the water, despite 'suffering from great weakness.'[27] Amongst the tributes, a medical officer described how the Rev. Cowl would be missed as the men of his Battalion had become good friends with their Padre and they greatly admired him, for he had put himself at risk spending much time in the trenches and not further back out of harm's way.

At the Central Buildings in Westminster, the Wesleyan Army and Navy Board discussed the Wesleyan war casualties to date and reported in their minutes on the latest news and progress of their Army Chaplain, the Rev. H.B. Cowl. The meeting minutes noted the following:

> The Rev. H.B. Cowl was wounded behind the trenches. When being sent from hospital in France for further treatment in England, he was on the Hospital Ship 'Anglia', which was mined in the English Channel. The Board rejoices that Mr Cowl escaped with his life. The Secretary was instructed to write to Mr Cowl, expressing the sympathy of the Board with him; and also to his father, the Rev. F.B. Cowl.[28]

Among the numerous condolence telegrams received by *Anglia* survivors and their families, was one written by Lord Stamfordham (Private Secretary to King George V) on the Monarch's behalf:

> The King is shocked to hear that the hospital ship ANGLIA which so recently conveyed him across the channel has been sunk by a mine adding an expression of heartfelt sympathy with the families of those who perished.

It is likely that the loss of the *Anglia* and consequent public outcry caused the German authorities to issue a statement the following August that the British were utilising Red Cross hospital ships to convey troops from England to the continent. Thus allied vessels would be indiscriminately targeted and torpedoed. However, there was strong British official denial of these German allegations.[29]

27   *Birmingham Gazette*, 4 December 1915.
28   MARC, Minutes of Army and Navy Board meeting, 27 January 1915.
29   *Dover Express*, 11 August 1916.

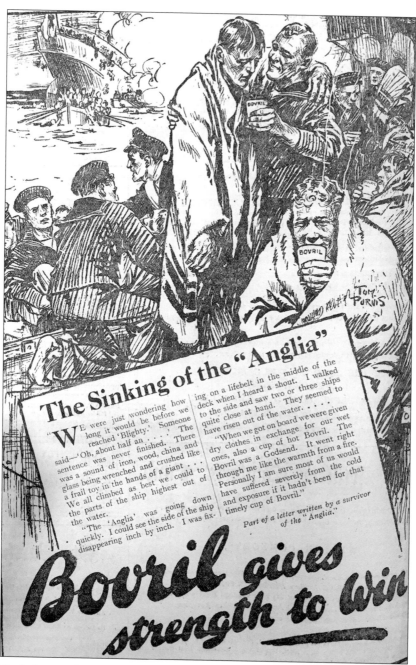

Patriotism, marketing and HMHS *Anglia*: Bovril advertisement of questionable taste published in many national newspapers shortly after the disaster. (Author's collection)

On 29 November 1915, a routine Medical Board Report recorded Herbert's numerous injuries:

> Place of Injury – Armentières on the 9th November 1915.
>
> The Board find – a shell-casing wound of face, scalp wound and wounds of hand.
>
> 1) Face – entry right side of face over lower jaw half way down 'anti' border of Ramus- septic. Large portion of casing passed through the jaw was removed from the opposite tonsil. Severe haemorrhage at the time. Compound 'comminuted' fracture of the Ramus and vertical fracture of the right side of lower jaw. Some three teeth missing. Portion of Ramus missing.
>
> 2) Scalp and hand wounds – was on board the SS *Anglia* when she sank. Owing to the explosion sustained scalp wound of head and hand. Scalp wound septic.
>
> Opens the mouth to admit the tip of a finger only.
>
> Recorded period for recovery 3 to 5 months.

Herbert was now deemed stable and safe in the hands of the doctors working tirelessly to repair the severely injured Army Chaplain. One specialist physician remarked, 'I can fix you and one day you will eat, but you will never be able to preach again!' His parents, sister 'Mukie' and her husband, James Trehane would have been hugely relieved to hear that Herbert was recovering and out of harm's way, but, as they all knew, there was one important person missing; the one needed most of all for a full recovery.

Without delay, Mr James Trehane, Herbert's brother-in-law, sent a telegram to North Vancouver, British Columbia. Addressed to the recovering patient's sweetheart 'May', then Miss Mary Louise Townsley – later to become my grandmother.

The telegraph simply read:

'Herbert survivor Anglia – very ill – London – Recovering – Come.'

Telegram sent to May Townsley, November 1915. (Author's collection)

7

Recovery

The exact duration of Herbert's stay in Beckett's Hospital is not known. However, the doctors at the hospital informed the War Office that Army Chaplain, the Rev. H.B. Cowl, would require an initial three months sick leave period to recover from his injuries. After such time a further medical review would be undertaken by doctors.

Whilst in hospital, Herbert had a number of visitors including his parents and other immediate family members. Able doctors gradually reconstructed his jaw and throat. During one of the many operations they inserted a silver tube into his throat in order to replace the damaged segment of windpipe – this was to change the sound and tone of Herbert's voice for the remainder of his life.

Christmas was fast approaching and Herbert was making good progress.

In Canada, the Townsley family would, no doubt, have been in turmoil. Although May had not seen her beloved Herbert for over four years, receipt of the telegram from Herbert's brother-in-law, would have left her desperate to return to England. However, she was the Townsley family's much loved only daughter and although both families knew May and Herbert were very obviously destined for each other, there had been no formal plans made for their future, as Herbert's commitment had always been first and foremost to the church and to his calling. The Townsley's two sons were already involved in the war – many Canadians and other British Empire men and women felt great pride with their new homelands but they also had great feelings for their mother country too. May's eldest brother, William Allan was already serving as an officer with the Canadian Expeditionary Force (CEF) in France and her youngest brother, Ernest Edward was serving on the Canadian home front.

Now the family were about to be affected further by the Great War in Europe.

May was determined to see Herbert and it was not long before the final decision was made and parental permission was granted with some reluctance, but also with their blessing. Thus the decision was made and she was to return to England to be by Herbert's side and ultimately to nurse him back to health. She left British Columbia for her solo journey across Canada and the United States before arriving at New York where she boarded the steamship SS *St Louis*. The journey was not a safe one for a young lady travelling on her own, so when the ship left the harbour at New York, May locked herself in her cabin for the duration of the crossing.

On the 22nd November, the War Office wrote to the Medical Officer in charge at the 'Hon. Mrs Beckett's Hospital' to review Herbert's health. The findings of the report noted, 'He is working to be fit for service under two months at the least.' A week later, on the 29th November, Herbert went to Caxton Hall in Westminster, to have his injuries assessed by the Medical Board who concluded that he would more likely need three to five months recuperation until he would be fit enough to resume his duties as an Army Chaplain.

In December, an article published in *The Methodist Times* entitled, 'A Tribute to the Chaplains' made special mention of one recently wounded on active service:

> One of our men at the Front pays a tribute to the devotion of Rev. H. B. Cowl. He says:-
>
> We are glad to hear that Mr Cowl is progressing satisfactorily; we shall always remember him. You will know that our chaplains have great difficulty in getting into the first-line trenches, but Mr. Cowl used to overcome all obstacles that prevented him getting amongst his lads in order to cheer them with his smiling face. We Wesleyans who know him and have already grown attached to him during the short time he has been amongst us, often have a little chat about him.[1]

Six days before Christmas, on Sunday 19th December, May arrived back in England. She had survived her Atlantic crossing without incident and her journey had come to an end at the docks in Liverpool. It is not known exactly where or how she travelled next, but she would have soon been on her way to London to visit Beckett Hospital!

Herbert's father was now the Minister at the Wesleyan Methodist Church on the South Parade in Sutton Coldfield, Warwickshire and he and Herbert's mother were living at The Manse in Anchorage Road. They had heard so much about May from their son that they felt they already knew her. Upon her arrival in England, they opened their doors and welcomed May into their family and their home. May lived with Herbert's parents at the Manse in Sutton Coldfield whilst Herbert continued his convalescence in hospital. They wrote to each other from Sutton Coldfield and Grosvenor Street.

On one occasion when perhaps Herbert was not feeling so well and optimistic, he wrote a very simple letter responding to her general points of news and then finished his letter with a fervent plea; 'My dearest love, Girl of my heart. I need your prayer. Herbert'.

Just before Christmas, Herbert was granted home leave.

On 21 January 1916 the Methodist Army and Navy Board held one of their regular meetings to discuss the ongoing situation of the war, the Army Chaplains and the

1   *The Methodist Times*, 9 December 1916.

Church's changing and evolving role within the armed forces. The second minute of the meeting referred to casualties and the first recorded update concerned Herbert:

Min.2. The <u>Rev. H.B. Cowl</u> is making good progress. The Board heard with much satisfaction that Mr Cowl is receiving a gratuity on account of his wound from the War Office Authorities.[2]

It is not known exactly when, but in the New Year, Herbert proposed to May and they began planning a simple wedding for the beginning of February. It was to be a relatively quiet event in view of Herbert's health, austerity and the country being very much preoccupied by war. Herbert was making good progress, but he was still unable to speak. However, that was not going to stop him from marrying the girl of his dreams!

On Saturday 5th February, the Rev. Herbert Butler Cowl and his sweetheart 'May', Mary Louise Townsley, were married by Herbert's father, the Rev. F.B. Cowl at the Wesleyan Methodist Church on South Parade in Sutton Coldfield.

Wesleyan Methodist Church, Sutton Coldfield where Herbert and May were married in 1916.
(Author's collection)

2   MARC, Minutes Armed Forces Board 1916.

May's family in Canada were unable to attend the wedding, but her uncle, Mr Thomas Townsley of Foggathorpe Grange, Yorkshire, performed the fatherly duties of 'giving her away'. The *Sutton Coldfield News* reported on the happy event; there was an account of the Rev. H.B. Cowl's war service to date, family backgrounds, and a description of the ceremony:

> The Chancel of the church was most beautifully decorated for the occasion, foliage plants and early spring flowers having been effectively disposed by the many friends of the superintendent minister. The latter himself performed the ceremony, and spoke a few brief words to the newly wedded pair. A former organist at the church, Mr F. Harpur, was in attendance and played several voluntaries, and the whole congregation – a fairly numerous one – joined in the hymns, 'Love Divine, all love excelling' and 'O Perfect Love'. The bride was given away by her uncle, Mr Thomas Townsley, and a London friend of the bridegroom, Mr Quarrington, acted as best man. There were no bridesmaids, the desire being to keep the ceremony within reasonably quiet limits; and the bride was dressed in the travelling costume in which she later left for the south. The bridegroom is, as a convalescent, on leave of absence for a few weeks only, and in that period the bride and bridegroom will spend time together at Torquay. They received quite a number of presents. From a few friends at the Wesleyan Church at Sutton, there was a handsome timepiece for the dining room, and another one for the study; while from the bridegroom's old friends at Bristol, and from many of those who knew him at Bournemouth in his younger days, when his father was stationed there, there were also tokens of remembrance and good will, including cheques and silver plate.

Also, *The Methodist Times* reported on the 'Chaplain's Wedding' giving details of the bride from British Columbia who had 'returned to tend and bring restoration.' This journal also described the chancel and communion table as; 'beautiful with choice flowers and greenery – "emblems of fresh youth."'[3] Little detail is known of the Torquay honeymoon, apart from the fact that, as a keen young photographer, Herbert took a number of photographs of the happy couple relaxing together, although no official wedding photographs appear to have been taken on their actual wedding day.

On the evening of Wednesday 24th February, Herbert and May were invited to attend a concert in Hotwells, Bristol.[4] The *Western Daily Press* observed, 'the chief interest lay in the promised visit of Captain the Rev. Herbert B. Cowl C.F. and his wife', and went on to describe the 'rapturous welcome' given to the Cowls at Hotwells:

3   *The Methodist Times*, 10 February 1916.
4   *Western Daily Press*, 26 February 1916.

His entrance to the school was the signal for a great welcome, the audience standing and cheering repeatedly. Musical honours and renewed cheers followed.[5]

The Rev. Samuel Body and the people of Hotwells had not forgotten the generous contribution Herbert had made at Grenville Wesleyan Chapel prior to the war. The newlywed couple were also presented with a silver tea set as a belated wedding gift by the grateful community.[6]

On the 29th February, a further medical assessment was carried out and another month of sick leave granted.[7] As per the bureaucratic process, the War Office requested monthly medical reports. Each month of sick leave was extended by a further month.

On 6 March 1916 King George V's Birthday Honours were announced and the Rev. Herbert B. Cowl had been awarded the Military Cross (M.C.) medal for 'Distinguished Service in the Field'. Herbert's exemplary gallantry on HMHS *Anglia* had been recognised. He was one of the very first Wesleyan Chaplains to be honoured with the Military Cross Medal. In the latter years of the war, there was a significant increase in the number of military awards issued to the Army Chaplains but at the beginning of 1916 there were very few military awards being presented to the clergy. By the end of that year, there were only 36 padres in the Army Chaplains' Department who had been honoured with the Military Cross.[8]

Fifty-seven-year-old the Rev. Theophilus Harris (Temporary Chaplain to the Forces, 4th Class), was the first Wesleyan Army Chaplain to be awarded the M.C. for bravery near Ypres at the end of 1915. Fifty-four-year-old the Rev. William H. Sarchet, a more senior chaplain (Hon. Chaplain to the Forces, 3rd Class) was the second Wesleyan Army Chaplain to be awarded the M.C. for 'service amongst the wounded'[9] and thirty-year-old Herbert (Temporary Chaplain to the Forces, 4th Class) was the third to be honoured thus.

Only one officer had witnessed Herbert's actions on that fateful day in November 1915. Herbert learnt in later years that had there been more witnesses, he would have been recommended for the Victoria Cross. However, due to the fact that he sought no glory or gratitude, this was of no great concern.[10]

Having returned from their honeymoon, the newlyweds spent time at Foggathorpe Grange in the East Riding of Yorkshire, staying with May's 90-year-old widowed grandmother, Mary Ann Townsley, and her uncle and aunt, Mr and Mrs Thomas Townsley. Grandma Mary Ann had six grandchildren who were serving overseas (as well as several great nephews and nieces), three of whom had left Canada to join the colours. Whilst recuperating, *The Selby Times and Howdenshire and Goole Advertiser*

5   Ibid.
6   Ibid.
7   TNA WO 339/47342.
8   War Office British Army Lists, Army Chaplains Department.
9   Wesleyan Minutes of Conference 1936, obituary.
10   Michael Cowl private recollections.

Herbert had a great love for books and during his convalescent period he would have spent many long hours reading. (Author's collection)

reported that although Herbert 'for some time had lay in a precarious condition', he was now 'rapidly gaining health.'[11]

The village of Foggathorpe, according to Herbert, was a delightful place, so it was with great pleasure that he continued his convalescence amidst the love and care of the Townsley family. On 16 March 1916 he remarked:

> … on Sunday evening next I am again to play the student: and (for the first time since November 7th) am to attempt to 'say a few words'.

He was invited to give an address on his war experiences at the Wesleyan Methodist Church Hall, Selby (approximately 10 miles from Foggathorpe) by the Young Men's Christian Association (YMCA), which was doing much good for soldiers and sailors. *The Selby Times and Howdenshire and Goole Advertiser* reported:

ARMY CHAPLAIN'S EXCITING EXPERIENCES WITH THE IMPERIAL FORCES – INTERESTING ADDRESS AT SELBY – WHERE TO FIND OPTIMISM

11   *The Selby Times and Howdenshire and Goole Advertiser*, 21 March 1916.

Despite being understandably nervous about his voice lasting for the full duration of the talk, Herbert was able to deliver the following address:

> The Chairman saluted the chaplain, who was working at the Front in the cause of their common religion, as a follower of the Prince of Peace, the Captain of their Salvation, and he saluted him in the name of their country as a soldier of the King, believing that they were fighting for righteousness, justice, honour, mercy and for peace, and believing that they would win.
>
> The Rev. Capt. Cowl, who was dressed in khaki, said that it was always a great honour to a man to stand and represent any great cause, and perhaps no honour had been greater than that which had been done to them as chaplains of their armies that day. To come back from the scenes where their sons and brothers were giving their best, and so many of them giving their lives also, and to try and bring back to them some message from them – some glimpses of their life, and if they could, to foster anew the spirit which inspired them, was what they were proud of. And yet there was one peculiar danger – a danger of exaggeration. They expected a wonderful story from them, and if they had lived there through all the months of the long war, and seen all its scenes as they had seen them second-hand through the papers, the story would indeed by thrilling in the extreme.

Herbert described many aspects of life from his short time on the front line, including his challenging role as an Army Chaplain:

> A chaplain, when he was there at home, had to be placed to a Methodist Circuit such as that was, but at the front they had first of all to find their circuit and it was no easy task, and after they had found their circuit, they had to reach it. It might be a broken-down cowshed or a half-ruined barn – it was generally an open field, and he had had to undertake his work standing on a manure heap in order to get a decent position to make the whole of the men who were there listen. In those strange places the Word of God was preached Sunday to Sunday. He could see as he looked into their faces the old familiar scenes in the place which was to him the most sacred. It was a poor sort of a church – on one side there was the old skylight in the roof of the barn or loft in which they were gathered, and on the other side there was a great opening which let in more air and draughts and heavy gusts of rain. There the men sat on the floor with their rifles and munitions, and with their faces besmeared with mud they had brought from out the trenches. There they sat and listened, and in moments like those a man had to be careful what he preached. There was no place for creeds, or sects, or theories – they must tell those men that there was a Christ in their midst – a Christ who belonged to them, and to whom they belonged, to whom they could reach out their hands and grasp his even while they were there, and were going back to the dread scenes of the trenches, and the message was – Be not afraid, because He is with you.

Herbert spoke fervently of days spent with the men in the front line trenches and the harrowing experience of the *Anglia* tragedy, before articulating the belief as to why his life had been spared:

> … he liked to think that the angel of God became his deliverer. He did not know whether they believed in angels or did not. He did. He did not want anybody else to do it if they did not want to. He would not insist upon it as a creed, but Providence was a personal thing, and was it difficult to make them see the personal that it became a guardian angel? They knew that Christ said that the angels always beheld the face of the Father which was in heaven. Was not He a guardian angel? He did not know what else it could be. He was unable to walk, but in that moment, by a very strange force, he was swung right on to his feet, and stood upright and he walked down the passage, holding on either side, into what seemed to be the last death stroke.

The article concluded with an account of the stricken hospital ship's last moments sinking below the waves in the Channel:

> … the boat went down under them and he was there until the last moment and went down with her for ten or twenty or thirty feet, and he should like to be able to bring back to them a message of those moments. After looking into the face of death, and standing at the door only waiting for admission and only knowing that the door was opened and that the Great Master was waiting – he wished he could bring back a message to everyone who was listening to him that day.

His honest and factual address had moved the people of Selby that Sunday afternoon.

On the 5th June, *The London Gazette*, the official public record, detailed the Military Cross award to one; 'Rev. Herbert Butler Cowl, temp. Chapl., 4th Class, Army Chapl's Dept.'

Herbert received notification on Monday 14th June detailing he was finally passed as medically fit to return to service, although because of the injury to his jaw and throat, he was deemed only fit for Home Service and not Overseas Service.

However, War Office paperwork confirmed that the Rev. Cowl was granted leave until 21 December 1916 and his gratuity would continue to this date, so once again this illustrated Herbert's desire to return to service as an Army Chaplain as soon as possible. An official confirmatory letter was sent from the War Office in Whitehall to the Rev. Bateson:

> The Secretary of the War Office presents his compliments to the Rev. J. H. Bateson, and begs to inform him that the Rev. H.B. Cowl C.F. has been transferred to the 66th (East Lancs) Division on Military Duty. He has been on sick leave.[12]

12   TNA WO 339/47342.

A further letter of instructions and an accompanying railway warrant (to be exchanged for a train ticket) were also received. Herbert had been appointed Acting Chaplain to the Forces, 66th (East Lancashire) Division, Colchester on the Suffolk and Essex border. The following day, on the 15th June, he wrote to the War Office from The Cups Family and Commercial Hotel, Colchester:

> I have the honour to inform you that I have this day – June 15th – reported to the 66th Division at Colchester.
>
> I have the honour to be, Sir, Your Obedient Servant,
>
> H.B. Cowl C.F.'[13]

In 1916 the 66th Division had moved to the south of England and taken responsibility for the defence of an area on the east coast.[14] However, most units were based at the Garrison and this is where Herbert was to spend the next few months.

Colchester had been a Garrison town long before the outbreak of World War One but when the war was declared Colchester suddenly witnessed a huge influx of volunteer troops. At its peak, the town had more than 20,000 troops stationed in the Garrison and thus doubling its own population.

The 66th Division was stationed at Colchester until such time that instructions were received for them to advance forth to France. These were nervous times as recent Zeppelin air raids on London and elsewhere in addition to disturbing rumours of possible German landings heightened local tensions. Correspondence from the Mayor's Parlour detailed the following:[15]

> An attempt at invasion is not at all improbable, and its temporary success is not impossible. It is therefore most necessary that the civil populations should be organised so that in the event of emergency they can evacuate the town with the least possible danger and discomfort to themselves. To avoid congestion it is earnestly hoped that the routes now given will be strictly adhered to.
>
> An order to evacuate the town can only be given by the Commanding Officer of the Army Defence ... Helpers wearing armlets of the same colour as the instruction cards will be posted at various points to guide inhabitants on the prescribed routes ...

Herbert was assigned to his new division where his ministry was stretched across the Garrison and into the town of Colchester. At the Wesleyan Church in Culver Street, located in the centre of Colchester, recreation was provided for thousands of soldiers

13   Ibid.
14   During 1914–16, the 66th Division provided trained replacements for parent units whilst carrying out home defence duties before embarking for the Western Front in early 1917.
15   My Wayside, Mrs Arthur Walters, 1930, London.

Herbert with the Rev. Arthur Walters at Colchester Barracks in 1916. (Author's collection)

stationed in and around the Garrison town. It was here that Herbert encountered a familiar face, Wesleyan Army Chaplain, the Rev. Arthur Walters, the husband of his cousin, Florence Susan Benjafield. Stationed in Colchester after being wounded at Gallipoli,[16] he was an un-attached Wesleyan Army Chaplain – not attached to any particular formation or unit.[17]

The church was so popular with the soldiers in Colchester that often the main church, hall, school room and parlour were packed to overflowing and often men had to be turned away. It was reported in the church minutes:

> Wherever the men go they remember this Happy Hour [time spent at Culver Street] and the many letters received from the Front testify to the memory of that gathering and the inspiration and good which came to them as they joined in singing the grand old hymns with which they have been associated from earliest years.

In July 1916 newspapers across the country reported that the German submarine UC-5 (which had laid the mine that sank HMHS *Anglia*) had been seized by the

16   Wesleyan Methodist Minutes of Conference, Obituaries.
17   Army Lists 1914–1918, Army Chaplains Department.

Herbert (second row from front, fifth from right, with May seated two places to his right; photograph taken outside the Wesleyan Church (demolished 2013) at Culver Street, Colchester. (Author's collection)

Royal Navy and was to go on public display along the Thames at Temple Pier. The U-boat had run aground whilst on patrol the previous April and her crew captured. This was an act of propaganda to help lift the morale of the British people on the home front. During the first hours of the first day of its public view, a large number of delegates from the Wesleyan Conference visited Temple Pier to view UC-5.

As the year came to a close, the 66th (East Lancashire) Division were ready to leave for active duty on the front line in France and Flanders. As Herbert was still classified as being unfit for overseas service, he had to leave the Division and be re-assigned with a new position in the Army Chaplaincy Department.

On 14 August 1916 a letter was sent from the Major-General, Commanding 66th (East Lancashire) Division to the Southern Army Assistant Adjutant and Quartermaster General, stating that 'The Rev. H.B. Cowl C.F. (Wesleyan) will report for duty at Portsmouth on Wednesday, the 16th instant'.

8

Home Service

In August 1916, Herbert was re-assigned to act as the Senior Wesleyan Chaplain[1] at the Portsmouth Garrison to replace the Rev. George Stuart Cann who was to be sent abroad on active service. Herbert and May moved into a small apartment at Blenheim House, 1 Clarendon Road, Southsea, Portsmouth in the autumn of 1916. The exact date of this move is not known, but Portsmouth was to become Herbert's base for the next two and a half years.

On Wednesday 13 September (on his 30th Birthday), Herbert attended the Portsmouth District Synod in Southampton, to take up responsibility for reporting on the Portsmouth Mission at Portsmouth Town Hall.[2] Also, he became involved in taking services and preaching at the King's Theatre in Southsea – the location was used as an extension to the Portsmouth Town Hall Mission.[3] However, this new role brought him into the barracks, hospitals and churches throughout Portsmouth and the surrounding areas.

The name Cowl would not have been unfamiliar to the people of Portsmouth as Herbert's father, the Rev. Frederick Bond Cowl, had been invited to the town to preach and attend various meetings on several occasions prior to the war. At the 1910 Leeds Conference, *The Methodist Times* photographed Frederick with a group of Methodist ministers entitled the 'Portsmouth District Representatives'.[4]

On the 20th September, Herbert attended his first Mission Committee meeting, held at the Duchess of Albany's Home (the name given to the Portsmouth Wesleyan Soldiers' and Sailors' Home). A week later, Herbert conducted a child's funeral service in Eastney (the south-east district of Portsmouth). Ronald Ernest, son of Regimental Sergeant Major Arthur Stratton, died aged 19 months old of tubercular meningitis. His mother, Agnes Louisa, wrote some years later:

---

1   *Portsmouth Evening News*, 26 August 1916.
2   MARC, Portsmouth District Minutes, 13 September 1916.
3   *Portsmouth Evening News*, 23 December 1916.
4   *Portsmouth Evening News*, 16 December 1899.

I lost my youngest child on 26 September 1916, two hours before his Daddie was killed in France.[5] His little body was laid to rest by the Rev. Herbert Cowl.[6]

It was in the town and harbour of Portsmouth that peace was broken on the night before young Ronald's death when a German airship, Zeppelin L31, the first and only one to be seen over the town, arrived overhead just before midnight. The civilian population was shaken when the night sky was filled with searchlights and defence fire. Zeppelin L31 dropped high explosives on her targets, most likely aiming for the harbour where a fleet of warships was stationed. On dropping the high explosives, the Zeppelin L31 increased height to escape from ground fire from the guns below; she disappeared into the night sky and was not seen again. Portsmouth was unnerved by the events of that night for days and weeks to come.

Three weeks later, whilst in Southsea, on Tuesday 17 October 1916 at 11.28 a.m., Herbert received a Post Office telegraph from London:

To: Rev. Herbert Cowl, 1 Clarendon Road, Southsea. Your attendance is required at Buckingham Palace on Saturday next the 21st inst. at 10.15. Army Service Dress. Kindly telegraph acknowledgement. Lord Chamberlain. Buckingham Palace, London.

On the morning of Saturday 21 October 1916, Herbert, accompanied by his father, made the journey to London and, at the Investiture ceremony in Buckingham Palace, His Majesty King George V bestowed the honour and decorated Herbert with the Military Cross medal. The award was given in the Sovereign's Birthday Honours' List and therefore a detailed citation was not recorded. The press and various publications announced the news. The next issue of *The Methodist Recorder* reported:

The Rev. Herbert B. Cowl, who was severely wounded in France, and whilst still suffering from his wounds narrowly escaped death by drowning, when the Hospital Ship 'Anglia' was torpedoed in the Channel, received his Military Cross from the hands of His Majesty the King at an investiture held at Buckingham Palace on Saturday last, Trafalgar Day.[7]

On the same day, 51-year-old Father Joseph Wrafter S.J. (Society of Jesus), an Irish Jesuit and Roman Catholic Army Chaplain, was also awarded the Military Cross.[8]

By the summer of 1916, only four Wesleyan Army Chaplains had been decorated with the honour since the outbreak of war. One of the Wesleyan Army Chaplains,

5   Ronald Ernest Stratton's father was killed in action during the storming of Thiepval.
6   Private Letter sent to Portsmouth Wesleyan Circuit by Regimental Sergeant Major Arthur Stratton's widow.
7   *The Methodist Recorder*, 26 October 1916.
8   *The Sunday Times*, 22 October 1916.

the Rev. Theophilus Harris M.C. was a Captain and the same rank as Herbert, a Temporary Chaplain to the Forces 4th Class. The other two recipients were Chaplains to the Forces 3rd Class, ranked as Majors. Therefore, Herbert was the second Wesleyan Army Chaplain of his rank to receive the M.C. during the war.

As the war progressed, and more military honours were awarded, it became increasingly difficult for the King to personally award the individual men and women at Buckingham Palace, so many of the ceremonies for honours were later conducted at army camps and at various locations around the country. A very high ranking army official would present the award, but Herbert had enjoyed the special experience of meeting the King in person and visiting the official London residence of the Monarch. As the war lengthened, more awards for gallantry were given due to the increasing size of the army and also as a morale boosting exercise, so during 1917 and 1918, there were a greater proportion of medals issued throughout the ranks and in the various theatres of war.

There was no mention of Herbert's Military Cross recorded in the minutes or agendas of the Wesleyan Methodist Army and Navy board. Given that so much was happening in the war, it appears it was simply overlooked.

Herbert's father, in a personal note dated 31st October, expressed his great pride in his son's award following the ceremony in London:

> My dear old Laddie, What a joy it was to me to see you and to be with you when you received your M.C.! I was gratefully proud of you dear boy. Your mother was so overjoyed at the thought of my being there.

Whilst May was with Herbert's parents at The Manse in Sutton Coldfield, it was obvious that she was beginning to fit in very comfortably with the Cowl family. Herbert's father wrote; 'Your "Little Girl" is all right. We are taking care of her and loving her and glad to have her.' In another letter, his father Frederick signed with his pet name 'Fadge' – writing again of their growing love and affection for May:

> We have been delighted to see May and should have kept her longer but for your sake. As she had to go north, we did not like to prolong her stay here. She is a dear child and we quite feel she belongs to us – you know that you can both come here just when you like for as long as you please.

Letters were frequently sent between father and son, day to day news, shared observations on life, practical family matters and happy memories of the past recalled. On a personal note, one of Frederick Cowl's other letters to his son typically concludes:

> I know how you will miss May but cheer up. She is on this side [of the Atlantic] and will soon return [to Portsmouth]. We think about you, talk about you, love you, pray for you.
>   Your 'Fadge'

The Rev. Frederick Bond Cowl, Herbert and sister 'Mukie'; photograph taken during Herbert's posting to Portsmouth. (Author's collection)

Although not an Army Chaplain, Herbert's father (like so many other clergymen) was also doing his bit for the war effort and was involved in the Sunday Parade Services at Sutton Park in Birmingham, where training and convalescent camps had been established.

In November, Herbert, still acting Wesleyan Army Chaplain on Home Service at Portsmouth with the Portsmouth Garrison and Naval Port Mission,[9] remained officially classified as being on sick leave by the military authorities. Once again, he felt his duty to serve God, King and Country was of the greatest importance. That month the War Office wrote to Southern Command asking for the Rev. H.B. Cowl to be re-examined by the Medical Board. As a result, his official sick leave was confirmed to the end of December. He continued to receive his gratuity from the War Office until this date, a period of more than twelve months. The recuperation progress had been somewhat problematic but, as reported in *The Methodist Times* earlier in the year, 'Recovery, slow and at times doubtful, has been mercifully granted.'[10]

9   MARC, Wesleyan Methodist Conference, Agenda 1917–1918.
10   *The Methodist Recorder*, 25 October 1917.

In the Army Chaplains' Department List of 1916, Herbert was one of only a dozen or so Wesleyan Army Chaplains who had the crossed sword symbol indicating service abroad denoting war service marked next to his name. He was also recorded as being one of only four Wesleyan Chaplains to be a M.C. recipient. Whilst at Portsmouth, Herbert was called to London on several occasions to see the Rev. J.H. Bateson (Secretary of the Wesleyan Army and Navy Board) who was the accredited Wesleyan Church representative to the then Secretary of State for War. It was during these meetings that they discussed matters concerning Wesleyan Army Chaplaincy and the on-going work at the Portsmouth Garrison and in the local Wesleyan community.

In January 1917, the New Year dawned with one question on everyone's mind – would the war end in the forthcoming year? *The Methodist Times* reported:

> The desire for peace grows stronger throughout the land as the meaning of war comes home to every family and the stress of conflict presses heavily on us all.

Herbert's work continued at the Portsmouth Garrison and the Naval Port where he was joined by two other Wesleyan Army Chaplains, the Rev. J. Henry Martin and the Rev. Robert E. Brown. Between them, they shared the work and responsibilities at the Garrison. At that point in time, the Mission comprised three main centres: Queen Street (Portsea), Town Hall and Eastney, with a smaller mission centre located at Clock Street, Portsea. The Rev. J.H. Bateson was also on the Mission committee and was actively involved in Portsmouth church affairs. Herbert became the Convener of the Committee which consisted of over 40 members comprising Chaplains to the Forces, ministers, philanthropists and local lay preachers. The Mission was involved in much good work including donations to the Home Missions, Foreign Missions, hospitals and the Poor Fund.

By 1917, May was with Herbert at Clarendon Road, living in their flat 'over Miss Best's milliner shop' as described by Herbert in one of his many letters to his parents. According to Wesleyan Methodist regulations, as a married couple, they should have been provided with a house, but in such wartime austerity, they were both very content with their cosy little rented abode. There were also times when Herbert's sister, Mukie (who was working as a Red Cross nurse in Dorset) would come and look after her brother whilst May visited her elderly grandmother in Yorkshire. Herbert's 'job description' appeared strenuous and diverse, as he was involved with the Royal Marines Barracks and the naval and military hospitals,[11] in addition to conducting nearby services at Eastney. In 1917 the Wesleyan Soldiers' Home there was no longer required and the Army and Navy Board issued instructions for it to be closed. The board reported, 'as the Eastney Home seems to have ceased to fulfil its purpose, immediate steps to be taken to close it.' The civilian congregation continued to use its rooms for the purpose

11   MARC, Wesleyan Methodist Conference, Agenda 1917–1918.

of Fellowship Meetings (previously known as Class Meetings[12]) and Sunday School although as Herbert recalled, the army had not entirely finished with these premises:

> One evening I entered that room for some week night meeting and there covering the floor and propped up against the walls, packed from end to end, side to side were wounded men just unloaded from the Western Front. They were the heroes of the hour and very well they knew it, but for all their pathetic disfigurements and their ghastly wounds, they were the gayest company I remember meeting.

Injuries ranged from small wounds to serious disabilities. Some injuries would be healed, however many men returned home from active service as pale shadows of their former selves.

At the end of February, the Portsmouth Mission commemorated its eleventh anniversary with a day of religious services that ended with Herbert preached to an evening gathering of 1800 at the Town Hall. This also indicates that Herbert's voice, although changed through surgery, was strengthening and that his vocal cords were well on the road to recovery.

Although still an Army Chaplain with priorities to attend to soldiers and sailors, Herbert found time for the local children too. During the following October, *The Methodist Recorder* reported:

> At the Town Hall children came over from the Duchess Hall (where they have their Sunday school at night) and filled the choir seats. Two hundred scholars sang the audience back to childhood. The hall was packed and hundreds were turned away before the time of service. Many stood all through and the Spirit of God was there.[13]

As one of three Wesleyan chaplains, Herbert had the freedom to adapt his role as local circumstances allowed. In an article in *The Methodist Recorder*, under the heading 'Extracts from Rev. J. H. Bateson's Letter-Bag', the Rev. Bateson observed:

> The heroism of faith often shines more distinctly in Hospital than upon the battlefield. The Chaplains in our home Hospitals may not see the glories of war, but they do see, from time to time, the glories of faith.

In October, Herbert was re-examined; this time at the Queen Alexandra Hospital in Cosham, Portsmouth. Again, the examining doctor reported that he was not fit for general service but was suitable for home duties.

---

12   Small group (approximately 12 people) meeting, usually weekly, for spiritual conversation and prayer.

13   *The Methodist Recorder*, 25 October 1917.

Herbert's sister 'Mukie', a Red Cross nurse, visited Portsmouth to look after her brother when May was away visiting her family in Yorkshire. (Author's collection)

As the months passed, so it became clear that a considerable number of Wesleyan Army Chaplains (as well as other denominations) were resigning their commissions. The war had proved to be a far greater challenge than many had anticipated. There were other wounded chaplains in a similar position to Herbert, who had been injured at the front and were working on Home Service or invalided from active service. However, for some, their new role as Army Chaplains had become too physically, emotionally and spiritually harrowing. A small number took advantage of their 12 month 'Temporary Contract' and finished their work after the single year of service. Others simply received official permission to resign and they returned to their local churches.

Herbert at times must have found his work very challenging and during these difficult times he sometimes showed a little self-doubt.

I find it a heavy strain. I am woefully 'out of practice', one gets sorely slack on one's more directly religious work in this ramshackle job here. But I guess it concerns a ramshackle workman rather than his job!

Herbert went on to describe the heavy toll of war:

One gets a bit alarmed these days; they buried just under the hundred here Saturday! They are now averaging 14 a day at Highland Road (all they can do in a day there) 30 at Kingston, and between the two at Stamshaw [Mile End Cemetery].

Despite the hardships there was a certain amount of flexibility with Herbert's role at the Portsmouth Garrison. In March 1917, guidance notes had been issued on service in the Army Chaplaincy Department which were distributed to all denominations.

There were times when Herbert found difficulties in his work with the decisions that were being made at a higher level in the church's organisation with regards to Army and Navy affairs. On one occasion Herbert wrote to his mother regarding his torment:

My staff arrangements are all upside down again! The Military Authorities have dropped on us, and ordered a reduction in cost by the removal of the 2nd full time chaplain. Meanwhile Brown, who went from Headingley when it closed, to Munitions has been ordered to join up on Thursday next! Bateson has been strafed by the President for bringing Brown here, and can do nothing for him. I have asked the President, over Bateson's head – to authorise an appeal for him, and if he will not do so, I shall strafe the President. If Brown goes, half our work here is 'in the air', and what we shall do I don't know. All I can say to Bateson and Co. is – 'Told you so! Ever since last Sept.!

But cheer up! There's life in the old dog yet!'

Although a little gloom and despondency were sometimes in the air, Herbert and May did find time to relax and enjoy each other's company. There were days when they could escape the troubles of war. On one occasion, Herbert wrote the following to his mother:

Our Forest picnic has at last matured, and is now one of the memories stored to sweeten winter days.

He also wrote a detailed account of their early morning start, the train journey to the New Forest and a leisurely morning walk to Lyndhurst under threat of impending rain:

On the edge of this wood we found a great buck-hole that gave us ample shelter from the rain. I cut a huge armful of bracken, made a couch of it, which I covered with my rain coat.

In the middle of lunch, with the fine view of moor and forest flung around on either side, and a leaden sky overhead, and none too warm a wind, we were suddenly struck with an inspiration; the ground was strewn with wood of all sorts, why not a fire? So in 10 minutes we had a fire roaring blaze! I found a tree stump that had gone to touchwood, which made fine solid fuel. And for the rest of the afternoon, as we rested and read, we had as merry a blaze as ever you welcomed on a cold winter's day! Maisie took off her shoes and stockings, which you will find in some of the enclosed photos, drying by the fire!

Then back to the Inn for tea; and comfortably home by the 5.25. Home by 8 o'clock.

So, despite a most unkind day, we had a real grand time! We enjoyed our bonfire immensely: brought back enough berries for one pie, a big bunch of glorious heather, and one or two photos of the Little Girl, worth (to my mind) all the journey!

On one occasion, Herbert was invited to a gathering at his old school, Cliff College, Calver in Derbyshire where over forty ministers were attending a week-long conference to review the work of the ministers / chaplains and the current state of affairs with the Wesleyan Church.[14] The different denominations were deeply concerned about the impact of war on membership. The gathering of ministers at Cliff College had been arranged as there was obvious general concern for the state of the Methodist Church by the time of the 1917 Wesleyan Conference. After many hours and days of discussion, self-appraisal and review, a report was produced for the 1918 Wesleyan Conference. *The Methodist Recorder* reported on 'The "Cliff" gathering and its findings', concluding; 'The Report has an "epilogue" about two subjects that remained unmentioned, yet present throughout – Education and Evangelism.'

However, there was no apparent action taken by the church as a result of the week long meeting at Cliff College.

Throughout Herbert's time at Portsmouth, he visited other places within the district, especially whilst attending meetings at Bournemouth, Southampton and the Isle of Wight, where he also visited the Horse Sand Fort.

Unfortunately, there was little opportunity for going to see his parents in Sutton Coldfield, but he regularly wrote to them and on a few occasions whilst in London Herbert was able to meet up with his father. Leave was considered a privilege and not a right.

In December, the Church President, the Rev. Simpson Johnson's Christmas and New Year's Message was printed in *The Methodist Recorder*. It began as follows:

We are approaching Christmas and the New Year in strange circumstances. Nation is up against nation; the area of conflict grows wide; homes are broken by sorrow and the world seems drenched with tears and blood …

It was a sombre message, but in the last months of 1917 there was hope of an end to the war; it was even being reported in the newspapers. However there was still nearly a year of suffering ahead. By early January 1918 the possibility of forming a League

14   *The Methodist Times*, 7 February 1918.

Herbert with binoculars in hand, on the seafront at Ventnor in May 1917; photograph taken whilst attending May Synod at Pyle Street, Newport, Isle of Wight. (Author's collection)

of Nations at the end of the war was being discussed. However, this was not to materialise and was not formally recognised until January 1920. Another year had passed and there was no end to the fighting and bloodshed, but a smattering of belief for a brighter future was now on the horizon.

The Wesleyan Army and Navy Board continued to report on Army Chaplain casualties, resignations, commendations, and new replacement recruits. In March 1918 it announced that the War Office had arranged the introduction of a School for Chaplains on Salisbury Plain – it would be an experiment, the first school of its kind.[15]

It was in late April, 1918 that Herbert wrote to his mother from Clarendon Road, Southsea:

Dearest Motherkin,
I don't think the war will last many months longer. I wonder when we shall be away from here!

15   Ibid., 28 March 1918.

Herbert assisting Boy Scouts with chores. Note the two wound stripes affixed
to his left sleeve. (Author's collection)

In the summer of 1918, Herbert was fortunate to be invited to preach at the Swanage
Sunday School Anniversary Service in Dorset on the Isle of Purbeck. This was a visit
to a special place from his childhood which was to become an extra special location
for him in future years. Closer to home there were other Sunday Service anniversaries,
including that of the successful Sunday School in Albert Road, Southsea. Herbert
gave an address to 700 children and friends of the church.[16]

Herbert was a great supporter of the work carried out by the Boy Scouts (The Boy
Scout Association). Many of the boys would help with air raid duties, coast guarding
as well as the guarding of important locations such as railway stations and telegraph
lines, helping in hospitals, and some of the older boys were trained in fire-fighting
duties. The Scout movement's contemporary *Official Handbook* (1910) detailed that
scouts should be prepared, if necessary, to 'die for your country if need be'.[17]

16   Ibid., 4 July 1918.
17   Imperial War Museum: Ten Ways Children Took Part In The First World War, Boy
     Scouts.

There were occasions when visiting preachers would come to Portsmouth and on one occasion Herbert recalled being amused by an unusual, impressive yet unlikely 'man of God'. He recalled:

> Gunner the Reverend Sir Genille Cave-Browne-Cave Baronet – it took some time to memorise. Gunner because in America he had enlisted in the Royal Artillery; Reverend because as a converted gunman he had become a minister in the Church of Christ and Sir Cave-Browne-Cave Baronet because he had recently inherited the baronetcy of that famous marked country family. I well remember his preaching the following Sunday in the Town Hall [Portsmouth Guildhall] to that great congregation mostly composed of men of the three services. How he stood on the platform without a note, pleading the cause of his master Christ. And how some time afterwards in the flat where we lived, my wife and I, over Miss Best's Milliner Shop at Handley's Corner, he told us the full story of his conversion – the moment in which that twinkling of an eye, his life was changed within and without.

After the war, the Rev. Sir Cave-Browne-Cave, 12th Baronet became a Church of England clergyman. Some years later he wrote an autobiography entitled *From Cowboy to Pulpit* in which he described his times in the non-conformist Church during the war:

> Here we had fine times in a Wesleyan Church. Real good earnest people, I like them; but some of their lay-preachers are remarkable, to say the least of it and some of their prayers are startling and their sermons wonderful.[18]

There was much good work continuing in the Wesleyan Methodist Church and many families continued to help with the Comfort Department. For instance, tens of thousands of pairs of socks were knitted and collected for the soldiers at the front. A new pair of dry socks was considered a luxury item as they were so greatly appreciated by a soldier spending long, cold wet hours in the trenches. Parcels of comfort sent to the front were often acknowledged by the Army Chaplains, and letters of appreciation and gratitude were often sent to the principal Wesleyan papers, *The Methodist Times* and *The Methodist Recorder*. Herbert encouraged the local people of Portsmouth to continue in all their great work supporting their men overseas.

At the Wesleyan Conference in July 1918, it was reported that there were now 262 Wesleyan Chaplains serving with the forces. Seven of these were acting Naval Chaplains and the rest were serving with the Army with 52 in home stations, 118 in France and Flanders, 12 in Italy, 16 in Salonika [Serbia], 28 in Egypt, 18 in Mesopotamia [Iraq/Kuwait], 5 in the Mediterranean stations, 1 in Holland, 2 in British East Africa, 1 on a hospital ship and 2 were prisoners of war.[19]

---

18   Rev. Sir Cave-Browne-Cave. *From Cowboy to Pulpit* (London: Herbert Jenkins, 1926).
19   *The Methodist Recorder*, 18 July 1918.

Also, by 1918 the church had become more structured with various booklets published to assist Army Chaplains. One of many topics included, 'Prayers and Hymns for Parade Services for use among Soldiers and Sailors of the Wesleyan Methodist Church', a pamphlet that was widely used in Portsmouth.

In October, Herbert's father Frederick wrote to him with the familiar usual mix of family news, but also wrote about the increasing tensions in Berlin (which were in fact the waves of discontent brewing at the beginning of the German Revolution):

> We are doing 'better' in the war at last. There is some hope that we may be out of it next year at this time. Not much before. The present move from Berlin is a 'booby trap' and nothing else. I have no confidence whatsoever in it. So long as their army keeps together and fights – as it is doing now they won't come to terms. [sic] And to defeat their army will take months.

Fortunately, his predictions were decidedly incorrect.

On the 11th hour of the 11th day in November 1918, the ceasefire came into effect, the Armistice was signed. The Great War was over, although a formal state of war between the two sides continued for another seven months until the signing of the Treaty of Versailles in June 1919.

In Portsmouth on that day – Armistice Day, Herbert stood in the Wesleyan Chapel, Arundel Street, Southsea to conduct the marriage ceremony of a young soldier from the Royal Engineers, Private Alfred Cole, to his sweetheart, local girl Olive Clarissa Holden.

Like many cities and towns across the country and across the world, Portsmouth celebrated the end of the hostilities. A large crowd, amounting to an alleged 40,000 people gathered outside the Town Hall in the square and in the surrounding streets, where men, women and children were giving praise and thanks for peace to a weary world. Relief soon turned into rejoicing and the subsequent cheering, applause and singing would have been deafening. Portsmouth was celebrating the end of four years of war.

The Methodist Recorder reported:

> The President of the Wesleyan Conference sent the following telegram to the King on the signing of the Armistice:- H.M. the King:- The Wesleyan Methodist Church sends, though its President, loyal and affectionate congratulations on this glorious and historic day, and unites in thanksgiving to God who has given us the victory. The President has also telegraphed the Prime Minister:- The Wesleyan Methodist Church sends, through its President, heartiest congratulations on the glorious and historic day, and unites in thanksgiving to God Who has sustained you through these arduous years and given us the victory.

Post-armistice societal changes were already noticeable when less than one month later, when Leading Army Chaplain, the Rev. Owen Spencer Watkins, recently promoted to Brigadier-General, became the first Wesleyan to be received at the Vatican by Pope Benedict XV.[20]

On Christmas Eve 1918, *The Methodist Recorder* gave a pensive thought for the forthcoming peaceful holiday season:

> Christmas returns once more and once more the world has rest from war. The four years during which the waters of a full cup were wrung out to us have passed; the desolating slaughter of young men and men strong in their prime has ceased. In that supreme consolation we may all gather some contentment, much hope, and a little leisure for wounds to heal. There is no haunting dread that, while we sit at such feast as we may be able to provide, many we love go in jeopardy of their lives.

Once the war was over, the Wesleyan Church helped the War Office with support for the men during demobilisation by providing them with assistance as their lives as soldiers ended and they returned to civilian life. Millions of veterans had to face the new challenges of adapting to a non-military existence and the church played an important role in helping the men to adjust to their new lives.

The 'After-War Committee' of the Wesleyan Royal Navy, Army, and Air Forces Board called upon its ministers, church workers and members generally, to take on the responsibility and exceptional opportunity that the end of war would bring to the church. The return of their soldiers and sailors to civilian life would bring many challenges but the church would be there to help and provide support for them in their communities.

The Army Chaplain's Department in Northern Command issued a visiting card for the Presbyterian, Wesleyan and United Board Chaplains to hand to their soldiers once they were demobilised. It is likely that Southern Command would have issued the same or similar card.

The front of the card read:

> Wish you God's Blessing now that you are returning to Civil Life.
> They thank you for all you have done in the cause of Liberty and Righteousness.
> And they pray that you many long be spared to serve God and work for the home which you came forward to defend.

On the reverse of the card it was detailed with the soldiers name and stamped with the date on which the soldier left the armed services:

20 *The Daily Mail*, 11 December 1918.

Portsmouth Guildhall – location of Portsmouth Mission, where Herbert spent much of his time taking services in the last years of the war. (Author's collection)

SHOW THIS TO YOUR MINISTER AT HOME.

Sir,
We earnestly recommend to your attention our friend who, after serving in the European War, is now demobilised.
    Yours faithfully,
    THE CHAPLAINS OF THE DEPARTMENT

The 'After-War Committee' thanked everyone in the church for the support of the soldiers' welfare during the war which included the conversion of school buildings, class-rooms and the building of Wesleyan Soldiers' Homes both at home and abroad. They commented on the chaplains – their life and example, their comradeship, courage, resourcefulness and readiness to help. The chaplains had won the confidence, esteem and even affection, not only of their own men, but of thousands who were not even declared Wesleyans.

    On Monday 7 April 1919 at 4 pm, Herbert attended his last meeting of the Portsmouth Mission. At the following meeting in June it was minuted, 'the thanks of the mission were heartily accorded to Rev. H.B. Cowl' for 'fine services to the mission during his ministry in Portsmouth'.

At the end of May 1919, Herbert was invited to the Wesleyan Church in Wells, Somerset to preside at the service for the unveiling of a stained glass window and two commemorative brass tablets in memory of the members of their congregation who had made the supreme sacrifice during the Great War.

Herbert gave the sermon and led the prayers. They all gave thanks to Almighty God that the war was over and that a lasting peace was in sight.

The *Somerset and West of England Advertiser* reported:

> Mr Cowl was speaking with some difficulty owing to the nature of his wounds, completely captivated and charmed the audience with his thrilling experiences at the Front and general Army work.[21]

As the summer months passed, Herbert continued his work in Portsmouth.

On 9 July, the city celebrated the end of the war and the official signing of the Treaty of Versailles with a Peace Pageant. As so often the case, the celebrations centred on the Town Hall [Portsmouth Guildhall] Square. The carnival atmosphere lasted the entire day and well into the early hours of the following morning. Red white and blue lights had been installed on the Town Hall, and searchlight beams of light illuminated the building converting it into a focal point for night festivities – the highlight being the unveiling of a light feature beneath the dome that read 'PEACE'.

Herbert had been on the Daily Posting List of Chaplains on 30 July 1919 detailing him to be demobilised. However, the arrival of the new chaplain, the Rev. Alfred B. Sackett from Gibraltar had been delayed and the Rev. J.H. Bateson had written from the Wesleyan Royal Navy, Army and Air Force Board (its title having been changed at the end of the war) of Central Buildings, Westminster, asking if Herbert could stay on a little longer at the Garrison until the new chaplain arrived. Herbert remained at Portsmouth until September 1919.

At the end of 1919, the Royal Army Chaplains' Department carried out a review of its role during the war and the lessons that could be learnt for the future. The review was entitled; 'An Enquiry and its Bearing upon the Religious Life of the Nation'. A committee was set up, with members of all the churches and theological institutes brought together to share their findings and views. There were three main topics listed for consideration; 'What the men are thinking about Religion, Morality, and Society', 'The Changes made by the War' and 'The Relation of the Men to the Churches'. There was analysis in all areas including; The Moral Impact of the War and The Church and Peace. However, nation-wide post-war attitudes were mixed with some experiencing a corresponding disillusionment with religion holding almost a sense of rebellion against God.

21   *Somerset and West of England Advertiser*, 6 June 1919.

Herbert's war had come to an end. He received news that his first civilian posting would be, as the school chaplain for Wycliffe College, with the Mid-Gloucestershire Mission Circuit in Stonehouse.[22] Following this appointment, Herbert and May duly settled into the Wesleyan Manse at Brightville in Stonehouse.

Approximately 530 Old Boys from Wycliffe College had served during the war. Of these, 77 boys had laid down their lives.[23] The newly-carved wooden chapel pulpit was dedicated to the memory of one of these old boys, Frank B. Vivian Thomas of the Duke of Cornwall's Light Infantry, although all the boys from the school who had not returned from the battlefront were remembered and honoured.

There was great excitement about Herbert's pending arrival at Stonehouse which was reported in *The Wycliffe Star* in August 1919:

All who know Mr Cowl congratulate us on this appointment. He greatly distinguished himself in the army, and we are told that as a chaplain he soon won the esteem of officers and men. He was most popular with the rank and file, for he always insisted on going with them into the front line trenches and sharing their lot. No danger deterred him. He was very seriously wounded with shrapnel in the neck. An operation was necessary immediately, and then when he survived they feared he would not speak again. Whilst so seriously wounded, he was on his way back in the hospital ship 'Anglia,' which struck a mine. The nurse and orderly at his bedside were killed, and he was frightfully knocked about, but in spite of his perilous condition he got on deck and put forth herculean efforts to save others from drowning, helping to construct rafts, etc. He stuck to the ship, hard at work all the time, till she sank in half an hour. He went down with her, but came to the surface and swam to a raft, and was picked up by a patrol boat and landed in an exhausted condition. For such bravery he got the M.C.[24]

Within a few months, Herbert had made his mark in his role as a Methodist minister with May at his side. Three months later, a school boy at Wycliffe wrote the following account in *The Wycliffe Star*:

Although Rev. Herbert Cowl, M.C., has only been known to Wycliffe boys for three months, he has already found a path to many hearts. The first thing that impressed us was his brevity. His first two sermons averaged eighteen minutes each, and his first address at prayers lasted four minutes. This amazing and ever-to-be-welcomed record has been fairly maintained. The next thing that impressed us was his 'chumminess,' with small boys as well as big, and his general interest in everything that interests us. Next came an impression of his ability, not only as

22   MARC Wesleyan Methodist Conference Agenda 1919.
23   W.A.S. & J.D.N., *Wycliffe and the War* (Gloucester: John Bellows, 1923).
24   *The Wycliffe Star*, August 1919.

a preacher and speaker but as a thinker. What he says is always worth saying, and he says it well. Other and perhaps even more vital things have impressed us too, but we already know Mr Cowl well enough to feel that, if he reads these lines, he is wishing that our head were handy in order that he might throw at it one of his many books, so we will simply say how glad we all have been to welcome Mr and Mrs Cowl to Stonehouse and to Wycliffe.[25]

The war was over and life was beginning to follow a new and welcome normality. In the spring of 1920 three young masters joined the school directly from the army. With the school having lost so many young men during the Great War, it was understandable that at times feelings were strong with regards to Britain's on-going relationship with Germany. On more than one occasion, there were debates in the school in relation to the 'policy of friendliness towards Germany'. It was always a close and heated debate. Some argued:

> The Germany of the old regime had passed away. Those who ruled in Germany to-day were democrats like ourselves. It was a great English principle never to hit a man when he was down. Germany was down, almost hopelessly so. It was neither generous nor just for us to sit on all her hopes and aspirations and to despise and reject all her advances towards a friendlier state of things. There was good in Germany as there was in us all, and we ought not to refuse to give it the chance of growth.[26]

Whilst others in the school expressed opposing views:

> It was up to us to capture German trade, not to give it back. Germany had deliberately provoked the war for material ends, and ought to be punished and to suffer. She had staked her all on a great gamble and had lost. Our devotion to what was right and clean and true must lead us to hate Germany.
>
> How was it possible for any decent person to shake hands with murderers, pirates, bullies and sneaks? The change of front in the German people between November 10th and November 12th, 1918, was too sudden to be really very praiseworthy
>
> … was the bloodshed in the war shed in vain?[27]

As emotions ran high, the Rev. Cowl would balance the debate, 'The atrocities and crimes of Germany had been great, but their ultimate punishment was at the hands of a higher tribunal.' It was understandable that feelings were still very raw, as so many

---

25   Ibid., December 1919.
26   Ibid., December 1919.
27   Ibid.

boys and young men from Wycliffe and Stonehouse had been killed during the war. The final haunting note made at the last debate on the subject read:

> Germany had stabbed us in the back in the past, and if we trusted her now we should be caught napping once again.

On 11 November 1920, the country remembered the war dead two years on. *The Wycliffe Star* published the following:

> On November 11th the Rev. H.B. Cowl, M.C., conducted a simple yet beautiful service in memory of the honoured dead. He spoke a few words concerning the ceremony then taking place at Westminster, after which we knelt in silence whilst the organ played the Last Post. As we knelt we saw again those gallant lads who went so simply to their grave; we heard again the Cease-fire buglers ring out over those long miles of riven land …[28]

On the Sunday before Christmas, General Bateson visited Wycliffe and attended the Foreign Missionary Meeting where the President of the Literary Society declared that 'some expression of gratitude' was due to the Rev. Cowl:

> There is not a boarder at Wycliffe who does not regard him as a friend–many would put it more strongly–and all are in his debt for the sermons and addresses, so brief, so earnest, and so eloquent, so charged with lofty thought expressed in pregnant phrase, that more than one boy has expressed the wish that he might possess the letter as well as the spirit of Mr. Cowl's speech, to carry with him all through life.[29]

Herbert most certainly did not forget what happened during the war and his views would have reflected those which were recorded in the Minutes and Agendas of the Wesleyan Methodist Church Army and Navy Board during the war, when the following 'Resolution' in respect of the fallen was to be submitted to the Conference:

> That the Conference of the Wesleyan Methodist Church places on record its admiration and appreciation of all sailors and soldiers who, having endured hardship and suffering, have laid down their lives. In the beauty of youth and the fullness of manhood, counting not their lives dear unto them, they have made the supreme sacrifice. Their virtues have won our admiration; the story of their heroism has thrilled our hearts. Their character and devoted service have won our undying gratitude.

28   Ibid.
29   Ibid.

To all who mourn their loss, bereaved parents, brothers and sisters, sorrowing widows and fatherless children, the Conference expresses its deep and affectionate sympathy. Earnest supplication is made continually that the comforts of the Father of Mercies and God of all Comfort may abound to their sorrowing hearts.

At the end of the war the Wesleyan Church proposed several schemes to mark the sacrifice and contribution made by the Wesleyans during the hostilities. A report by the Army and Navy board recommended:

In view of the fact that the casualties of the war included nearly 25,000 Wesleyans who have been killed in action or died of wounds and sickness, it is felt that a permanent memorial would be a fitting tribute to their heroism and devotion to duty.[30]

In subsequent years, the church introduced many memorial projects including the erection of a new Garrison Church at the Catterick Camp in Yorkshire. Princess Mary attended the 1928 dedication with many of the church and army hierarchy present.[31] Thousands turned up for the official opening. Two large stone panels embedded in the church exterior stated:

To the Glory of God
And in memory of
the 26,581 Wesleyan Sailors, Soldiers & Airmen
who laid down their lives in the Great War 1914 – 1919
and
To the Glory of God
And in memory of
The 31 chaplains, ministers and students
who laid down their lives in the Great War 1914 – 1919

As a result of his injuries in 1915, Herbert was unable to speak of his experiences of the war at that time. However his memories and recollections were written down to be shared with those who were close to him. After the war, those memoirs were safely filed away and the years passed, until they were re-discovered nearly a hundred years later by his granddaughter, the author of his story, '*The Half-Shilling Curate*'.

---

30   MARC, Minutes Armed Forces Board 1919.
31   *Gloucester Citizen*, 9 August 1928.

9

The Final Chapter

The difficultly in writing is to know how much not to say: for my yarn, fully told, would be a long telling.

The experiences of the year have been a great privilege, though I shall not take the worthy ex-president's advice and make at least 3 or 4 lectures out of them!

I found the duties of a chaplain at the front to be a great problem. Parade Services on Sunday, and funerals whenever called on to conduct them, define the full limits of one's military duties. To find scope for one's ministry beyond that, was to me the real problem.

One could live back with the Field Ambulance Head – Quarters, make the occasional visit to the firing line for a funeral, and take Sunday's work and so live easily and comparatively safely.

However, I felt it necessary to get into personal touch with my men; so went up to live at the Advanced Dressing Station, 50 yards outside the trenches, and right in the artillery area. For some weeks I spent most of my time in and out of the fire-trench.

You can get at a man on his own ground, as it were, if you go to him and smoke with him in a dug out in the fire-trench. And if it is my privilege in the future to return to the fighting front I shall not hesitate to continue the same methods I believe that in time I could have accomplished much for Christ in this way.

Yet, I still hold that the greatest opportunity for winning men for Christ is in the Home Camp before they set out for the front. Speaking from my own very limited experience, I found no added religious impressionability amongst the men I came in contact with out yonder. Before starting for France, I was seeing a slow but steady work of conversion amongst the men. In three months of work at the front I was not aware of any particular instance of conversion.

It is not known to whom this letter was sent or who received it. It was simply addressed – 'Dear Old Chums.' In March 1916, following Herbert's first extraordinary year as an Army Chaplain and whilst he was convalescing at May's grandmother's house in Foggathorpe, he recollected and reflected on his experiences as a padre at the front line.

Herbert with his father, the
Rev F.B. Cowl at Swanage
Bay Lighthouse, Dorset.
(Author's collection)

Herbert ends this letter with the following lines:

So, here I will stay my very rambling and weary pen.
    We at Foggathorpe bless you all with all our hearts for your thrilling letters.
And especially my wife joins me in heartiest greetings to each of you, to whose
fellowship I am proud to be spared, and she is proud to be introduced.

'The Half-Shilling Curate' – In this story, through his recollections which are supported
by copious correspondence, we learn that The Half-Shilling Curate was a loving
Christian man who wanted to be a good and worthy Wesleyan Army Chaplain.
Perhaps in those early days in 1914-15, he felt that his inexperience was holding him
back. But who would have been prepared for anything like the war that was unfolding
in Europe? The Wesleyan Church, along with other religious institutions was finding
its feet. Even the War Office was uncertain regarding the value of the Army Chaplain
at the onset of the First World War. However, as the war proceeded, their numbers
substantially increased as the military authorities and the Church together realised
the important contribution the Army Chaplains were making to the war effort.
    The Army Chaplaincy Department increased substantially during the war. In
August 1914 there were only 117 chaplains (none from the Wesleyan Church); in

August 1915 there were 1,164 chaplains (100 from the Wesleyan Church) and by August 1918, there was a total of 3,416 chaplains (256 of them Wesleyan). Never before had so many clergy donned uniform to provide succour for the troops.

Some chaplains may have felt that there was little for them to do in those early days of the war, but in Herbert's case, he always kept himself busy – defining his new job and being totally committed to his vocation and supporting the men in 'his' battalion. The Army Chaplain's job description had in effect developed and changed – not only were they involved in the denominational support of their respective faiths, but they were also expected to provide a more general pastoral, spiritual and caring role. So, from 1914 to 1915, it would be easy to understand how, with perhaps limited guidance, Herbert felt like 'The Half-Shilling Curate'.

From those early days at Bordon Camp in Hampshire when he first heard jeering during parade services and experienced universal resentment from the men he was trying to help, to the correspondence from soldiers who missed his presence in the trenches (received after he was wounded and returned home), Herbert had found his true vocation and finally earned the deep respect of the men he so passionately wanted to help and serve both overseas in the front lines and in the Army Garrisons at home!

There are those who believed that the Army Chaplains of the First World War kept out of harm's way – enjoyed a safer existence further back from the front line and perhaps this was true in some cases. Robert Graves, poet, scholar, novelist, agnostic and soldier in WW1 voiced his opinions with biting and withering comments regarding the role of the chaplains. However, there is now plenty of evidence to contest Graves' view on their value during the Great War. Herbert's war experiences are testimony to the work of a practical chaplaincy fulfilling a much greater challenge than simply being in-situ and not risking their own lives.

In Herbert's story, the book title 'The Half-Shilling Curate' refers to the pet name by which he corresponded with his parents during his early days of military service. This was a humorous twist regarding his youth and inexperience, in the expression, 'not being the full shilling' meaning, 'he's not the full shilling, but a damn good worker!' It was a slang phrase meaning someone a little unintelligent or slow, but this was definitely not the case regarding Herbert! He so wanted to be a good and valued Army Chaplain for God, for those in his care, for himself and for his parents. Ironically, it is interesting to note that there was no such coin as a half-shilling, before, during or after the Great War. Also, this point illustrates Herbert's great yet subtle, sense of humour! Perhaps those early insecurities were manifested in the signature on his letters home; 'from your loving son, The Half Shilling Curate, Herbert'.

However, his faith in God was strengthened, not lessened, as a result of his war experiences, both from duty in England, France and in Flanders.

Herbert would have learned to address the different religious dynamics, including the careful navigation through other denominations, of class, gender, war, patriotism, ethnicity, regionality and age. One of the main challenges he had to overcome in fulfilling his role as an Army Chaplain, was the balance of preaching the national cause and, at the same time, sharing his Christian beliefs. However, despite all these difficulties, there is no doubt that if Herbert had recovered fully from his injuries, he would have eagerly returned to the front line to serve alongside the soldiers once more as an Army Chaplain.

By the end of the war, approximately 180 Army and Navy Chaplains had lost their lives including; Wesleyan Methodist, Primitive Methodist, Congregational, Baptist, Presbyterian, Anglican clergy and Roman Catholic priests. They were killed in action, suffered illness, died from wounds or disease – they had all made the ultimate sacrifice for their God, King and Country.

It is arguably the case that between 12 November 1918 and 31 August 1920, a further 20 Chaplains died as a result of injuries and illness related to their service in the war.

On a personal note, at the end of the war in 1918, Herbert had lost two of his first cousins. Many of them had signed up to the war effort but Charles Frederick Butler and Howard Richard Henry Butler paid the ultimate price of war. Charles and Howard (aged 20 and 21) both died in separate flying accidents in 1918 whilst serving with the Royal Flying Corps and the Australian Flying Corps respectively. Two other relatives, brothers, an Anglican Army Chaplain, the Rev. Wilfred John Harding died at Passchendaele whilst retrieving wounded soldiers from 'no man's

Herbert, Minister and School Chaplain at Wycliffe School c.1919. (Author's collection)

land' in 1917 and Capt. Reginald William Fowler Harding of the London Irish Rifles was killed in action seven days later whilst fighting in Palestine (Jerusalem).

The war years had finally come to an end. Herbert was now a civilian and had returned to his life as a Wesleyan Methodist minister enjoying his work for the Church with May at his side. His work in the ministry continued at Stonehouse and at Wycliffe School in Gloucestershire.

Herbert's sister's war had also come to an end. Muriel finished her work serving as a Red Cross nurse and reclaimed her pre-war life as a wife and mother looking after her husband and four young children, returning to the farm and market garden at Hampreston in Dorset.

At the end of 1919, May was pregnant and expecting their first child the following summer. On the June summer solstice 1920, Herbert and May became the proud parents of a daughter, named June Yeoman Cowl.

In September 1921, a letter was sent to the Rev. H.B. Cowl at Stonehouse from the War Office in London:

> Sir,
>
> I am directed to inform you that in recognition of the services rendered by you in the Royal Army Chaplains Department, approval has been given for your appointment as an Honorary Chaplain to the Forces, 4th Class as from 1st Sept. 1921 on which date your commission as a Temporary Chaplain to the Forces ceased to have effect.
>
> In this capacity you will be permitted to wear uniform when attending ceremonials and entertainments of a military nature, and on occasions when the wearing of uniform would appear appropriate. In the event of your being called upon to conduct religious services for troops, the Chaplain's Scarf may also be worn.
>
> The uniform will be restricted to service dress and the badges of rank will be those of your honorary rank. The letter 'R' will be worn on the collar below the collar badges. This order is not to be interpreted as granting permission for the wearing of uniform generally and on all occasions; uniform may only be worn as directed in paragraph 2. Uniform may not be worn at meetings of a political nature.

At the end of the school summer term 1922, Herbert's time at Wycliffe came to an end. There was great sadness in the school and *The Wycliffe Star* reported on his leaving:

> From the oldest to the youngest, all at Wycliffe mourn the fact that, when the School re-assembles in September, the Rev. Herbert Cowl will have gone from our midst. We have never had a more popular 'chaplain,' or one more loved.[1]

---

1   *The Wycliffe Star*, August 1922.

The Headmaster Mr W.A. Sibly reported:

> I would like – unusual though the place may be – to take this opportunity of saying how much we thank Mr. Cowl for all that he has done for us. Not only in the services which he has taken here, but in every way, by fellowship and inspiration, he has touched life to finer issues. He has shown us that the things of Christ are lovely, and that religion is a great and winsome thing. He has been a true ambassador of his Lord and ours, and some there be among us who cherish a desperate but daring hope that, in a day that is not far, he may come back to Wycliffe, here to help us still.

Herbert devoted his life to the church and to his family. As a Methodist minister he moved around the country from circuit to circuit and in the autumn of 1922, he was stationed at the Redland Circuit in Bristol where on Monday 12 May 1924 Herbert's family was made complete with the birth of their son, Michael Cowl.

Two years later the family lived in Mumbles near Swansea in south-west Wales, where they lived for three years. In 1929, after their time in Wales, they moved to Middle Lane in the Highgate Circuit of London.

The years passed by, but Herbert never forgot the people of Portsmouth or his time at the Army Garrison during the Great War, often returning to Southsea to preach at the local churches.[2] On one such occasion, the local newspaper commented on his humour which had not been forgotten. Whilst giving his sermon at the Albert Road Sunday School Anniversary celebrations in 1932, Herbert called for "trespassers to be persecuted!" When he discovered his mistake he added, 'I should say 'prosecuted'. Never mind, they both begin with 'P".[3]

Also, in 1932 the three Methodist churches; the Wesleyan Methodists, the Primitive Methodists, and the United Methodists joined together to form one church, the Methodist Church.

During Herbert's ministry in north London, he worked with several notable ministers who had served with him as Army Chaplains in the First World War, including the Rev. Cecil Weeks who had been at his bedside in Boulogne at the end of November 1915.

In 1933 Herbert and May moved to the Finchley and Hendon Circuit in north London. Herbert became the new Methodist Minister at Hendon and was instrumental in the building of the new Hendon Methodist Church at the beginning of 1937.

On the 4th March of that year, Herbert's beloved father, the Rev. Frederick Bond Cowl, aged 84, passed away in his home at "Little Red House", 24 Eldon Road, Winton in Bournemouth. His father had been a great influence with his unassuming

2   *Portsmouth Evening News*, 4 June 1932 & 13 June 1936.
3   Ibid., 6 June 1932.

and modest ways. His father had been a founder of the Wesley Guild (part of the social and caring life of the Church) and a member of the Legal Hundred.[4]

In *The Record*, the Finchley and Hendon Circuit newspaper described the immense sense of personal loss:

> The Rev. F.B. Cowl was a choice spirit and many are happier and better for his example and counsel – he set waymarks for doubtful feet and kindled love for God. We have some little idea of what such a father has meant to such a son.[5]

Herbert's work as a Minister would often mean that he and May would be parted for short periods of time. However, when they experienced these periods of separation, they would often write to each other and Herbert still referred to May as his 'Beloved Girl':

> What a joy to look for your return! I can't tell you how I have loved you and missed you since you left! Isn't it wonderful to keep this unchanging love with all one's changing thoughts and circumstances!

By the late 1930s another European conflict appeared imminent, but it was not to be Herbert's war. He was 53 years of age and the upper age limit for Army Chaplains was 55. Herbert's war would be at home, in the community supporting the people of Ealing, Acton and North London. Before leaving Hendon, a church pulpit lantern and plaque was unveiled: 'In memory of Herbert Butler Cowl, who under God inspired the design and building of this church'.

After months of rising tension, on 1 September 1939 the Second World War broke out in Europe, and both of Herbert's children became involved in the war effort; June worked for the Home Office in the intelligence service and Michael, as soon as he was old enough, signed up to the Royal Navy. June and Michael shared the same sense of duty to King and Country as their father had shown and demonstrated many years earlier at the onset of the First World War. May was involved too – not only in supporting her husband with his pastoral work but she also took on the responsibility of becoming the President of the Church Working Party supporting the local coordinated mobilization of people's resources.

During the Second World War, Herbert and May lived at 5, Twyford Crescent in Acton. Herbert was the Methodist minister at Acton Hill, a large church with seating for over 900 people on the Uxbridge Road, from 1939 to 1945 and this is where he experienced first-hand the devastation of German bombing in the local boroughs, the Blitz in the Capital and the suffering of those affected by enemy action. On the home front he helped the local community with the preparations for war; the blackouts,

---

4   *Methodist Conference Minutes*, 1937 Obituaries.
5   *The Record*, April 1937.

food and clothing rationing, the digging of Trench Shelters in Acton, including one in the road they lived in.

Once again, the world was at war and, like so many men who had been part of the First World War, it was now time for Herbert to be the parent, the loving father anxious about his children and the risks and sacrifices that they might be taking for peace, righteousness and the freedom of Europe. Instead of writing letters home and reassuring his parents that there was no danger in his war, this time he was the concerned and worried parent waiting to receive the welcome letters sent home from his children. Times had changed and Herbert had to learn the pain of being a parent (just like his parents had endured during WW1) and the inevitable uncertainty and fear for the safety of his daughter and son, June and Michael.

At times it was extremely dangerous staying in London with the ever increasing threat of German action. Herbert embraced the home front challenges, drawing on his 1914-18 war experiences whilst providing support to the people of Acton, as they became more familiar with the real threat of enemy action. As people became more aware of the air raids and the reality of evacuation in the area at the end of 1939, Herbert worked tirelessly to re-assure those around him and he gave comfort to the members of his congregation. London was preparing for war. Children from the nearby schools in Acton were evacuated to Devon and May helped too by taking Herbert's two elderly nervous aunts, his father's sisters, from London down to Dorset out of harm's way.

Following a visit to see his family at Hampreston in Dorset at the end of May 1940, he wrote at the back of his sister's bible:

> May 29, 1940 – I wish to record a special memory. Last evening I went to tea at David's [nephew] and was thrilled with it all – home, flowers, children and all, and I thank God for such an oasis at such a critical time in our history – Read / Isaiah 40.v31 stands out.

The verse referred to was a passage from the Old Testament prophet:

> Those who hope in the Lord will renew their strength.
> They will soar on wings like eagles; they will run and not grow weary,
> They will walk and not be faint …

At the beginning of June 1940, Herbert even moved one of his more nervous and fragile parishioners, Edna Shaw and her two daughters down to his brother-in-law's home in Dorset. Prior to the war, the Cowl and Trehane families had taken a long rental on Clotten Cottage, a thatched cottage set in the heath of the Goathorn Peninsula on the Isle of Purbeck. The family used to spend quality time together enjoying the pleasures of the Dorset countryside. However, in 1939 the whole heath had been requisitioned by the British Army for training purposes and the cottage had to be abandoned to the war effort.

On one occasion in the summer of 1940, Herbert visited the Goathorn Peninsula – it is not known exactly where he stayed. In a letter to his son on 14 June, he wrote about the local countryside and its wildlife with his own distinctive personal observations, but then he wrote about the war on the south coast of England:

> There is a searchlight outfit right beside Dr Dangerfield's! At 6.30 this morning, the anti-aircraft was roaring away for half an hour over Southampton – I should judge.
>
> There are anti-submarine nets across the Harbour mouth, and quite a lot of troops in Sandbanks. And yet it all seems utterly peaceful. The gunfire was swallowed up by the tiny sounds of immemorial life around here – bird & bee & wind – croon in the pines.

Herbert considers the future of the war and later in his letter writes:

> No one can make any very definite plans just now: this island now becomes a fortress, with only one thing to do, – to defend itself. If we can do this for a couple of months, we should be in a position to make some plans after. Meanwhile, anything you can pick up about shooting, A.R.P. work, digging, driving, or anything of a practical sort like that – go to it! And don't worry about us. When the attack on England develops, you probably won't hear for a long time. But when we get any idea of its course, – then if Dorset seems to be relatively safe, I shall send your mother down there, and June too.

Herbert concludes his letter to his son:

> But we shall see. We don't believe in God because His is the winning side, or in the hope that He will screen us from trouble: but because His is the <u>right</u> side, and He fits us to <u>meet</u> trouble.

By the autumn of 1940, Acton was being hit badly by enemy action. The bombs continued to fall and in September 1940 a family friend wrote to Herbert enquiring if his 'address (and nerves)' were 'still intact'.

On Thursday 10 October, Herbert wrote to his son, now lovingly called 'Mike':

> I'm sitting in the Scout's Hall waiting for any soldiers to arrive who like to use it as a reading and writing room. All the empty houses in Twyford Avenue have been filled with soldiers: they have no light and no heat in the houses! So we want to make them at home along here. So far, I've been here for three nights and no one has turned up. They all know about it, but I expect they prefer cinemas and the more interesting streets. When we get to wet, cold nights, they may turn in. If not, we have done our best.

He went on to explain how, 'a fortnight ago I packed off the whole house' which included persuading May to temporarily move down to 'Simon's Ground' (a Trehane family home) in Hampreston, Dorset, to be with family.

Herbert's letter gave further detail regarding immediate dangers:

> Jerry is concentrating on railways and factories at present; and as we have a network of both, we come in for a lot of attention. Most nights you can tell what he is after, when he has dropped his first stick of bombs. (As it is, I'm writing badly partly because he is now circling round overhead looking for something: the shells are bursting continuously round him: and it isn't a nice business sitting alone in this cockle-shell building while he tries to make up his mind where to lay his eggs. When they do drop, they sound as if they are coming right on top of you, though they may be half a mile away, or more. And as he is mostly using 500 lb ones, you are sure your last moment has come, until you find you are still alive! We shall get much more used to it in time; but it isn't easy at first.)

More observations followed; the spotting of a Clouded Yellow [butterfly] at West Acton Station; a broadcast programme of a man enthusiastically talking about collecting Wills cigarette cards for botanists called 'Moths & Butterflies' and his deep appreciation of his most recently read books. Herbert concluded with observations on the close proximity of the war:

> I can't get away from here just yet; and doubt if I shall before Christmas. Your uncle is coming up for Milk Marketing Board on Monday, he says. I have written protesting that he ought not, and the Board should know better than to bring men in here at present. You don't hold meetings on a battlefield.
>
> (Heavens, what a racket! This room rocks with the crash of guns that seem close round us; the bursting shells above; and the throb of a fleet of Jerrie's heaviest stuff. But he has dropped only <u>one</u> bomb near here since I began to write: I guess he's having a very uncomfortable time up there!)
>
> All the best to you, Mike. You are always in my mind. And I know you will have a thought to me. You can thank God for the wonderful help he is giving me, and pray, – not that he will keep me safe, but make me useful.
>
> As ever, D. [Dad]

Acton was badly hit during the war, the Germans dropping high explosive bombs, incendiaries, mines, oil bombs, V1s – flying bombs, also known as 'Doodlebugs' – and other devastating explosives including phosphorous missiles.[6] There were thousands of casualties in the Ealing, Acton and Southall boroughs; Acton alone suffered 163 killed,

---

6   Maureen Colledge, *Tin Hats, Doodlebugs and Food Rations: Memories of Acton in World War* (Acton: Acton History Group, 2008).

Salvage work in Acton after German bombing in 1940. (Ealing History Centre)

290 seriously injured, as well as over 500 sustaining lesser injuries. Five hundred and twelve buildings (including houses) were destroyed and approximately 7,000 properties were damaged in varying degrees. Throughout the war, Herbert preached and served all the churches in the Circuit, covering Ealing [Broadway], Acton [Hill], Hanwell, West Ealing, Acton Green, Northfields, Pitshanger, Greenford, Northolt and South Acton, so he would have been very aware of the widespread devastation.[7]

Despite the destruction of war, Herbert's faith remained strong. Minutes from one of the 1940 quarterly meetings noted:

> He spoke of the marvel of being able to carry on quietly with the business of the Church while in the midst of such great calamity, and wondered if it came from complacency or through a feeling that the Work of God was supreme.[8]

7   Ealing History Centre: Ealing and Acton Circuit, Directory of Services.
8   Ealing History Centre: Ealing and Acton Circuit, Acton Hill Quarterly Meeting Minutes.

During the Blitz the work of the churches in the local boroughs was often affected by the bombing and 'the Work of God was postponed owing to Air Raid conditions'.[9] Through the latter months of 1940, bombing was constant with only occasional days of relative quiet before renewed German attacks.

In late November, a young Raymond Alastair Leader, hailing from the Acton Hill Methodist Church, was acting as a temporary Air Raid Warden. Severely wounded whilst carrying out duties during a raid on Gunnersbury, he died the same day in Acton Hospital.[10] Herbert knew the family well, Raymond Leader's father being a member of the church choir. Herbert and the previous incumbent, the Rev. J. Crowlesmith, conducted the funeral service with the coffin draped with the Union Jack; on the top lay a wreath and Brodie[11] steel helmet.[12] Six men from the ARP (Air Raid Precautions) carried the coffin down the church aisle. One of the victim's friends remarked to a reporter from the *Acton Gazette and West London Post* that 'he [Raymond] had signed up on his 18th birthday a month ago for the R.A.F., and had been sworn in two weeks ago and was waiting for call-up.' At the funeral, the organist played Bach's 'Jesu, Joy of Man's Desiring.' It was Raymond's favourite piece of music.

On 26 January 1941, Herbert received a letter sent from London and signed by an anonymous business man:

> Dear Mr Cowl,
> As one who lost his faith in God some years ago and now, as a result of the war, is in process of regaining it, I should like to testify to the help which I derived from your sermon this morning at the City Temple [a non-conformist church in Holborn]. There must be times when you feel discouraged and this letter is written in the hope that it will be remembered in such times. Incidentally, this is the first time I have written to anyone to thank him for a sermon.
> Our greatest hope today is that we should live surrendered, guided lives. The church, visable and invisable has a tremendous opportunity to act as heaven and I am sure that your influence will be important.
> My name doesn't matter so, wishing you every success, I merely sign myself,
> 'A Business Man'

Less than three months later, City Temple, the non-conformist church at Holborn Viaduct, was destroyed by German incendiary bombs at 2.30 am during an air raid on the night of 16/17 April 1941. Extending over eight hours, its primary target was central and south London. Over 1,000 civilians were killed on that fateful evening. The City Temple minister was Dr Leslie Weatherhead and the ghastly events of

---

9   Ibid.
10   *Acton Gazette and West London Post*, 15 November 1940.
11   Helmet used by Air Raid Precautions wardens during WW2.
12   *Acton Gazette and West London Post*, 22 November 1940.

Herbert with his friend and colleague, the Rev. Leslie Weatherhead who later became President of the Methodist Church. (Author's collection)

that night would have surely cemented the beginning of a close life-long friendship between Leslie Weatherhead and Herbert Cowl.

Acton Hill Church did not suffer direct bomb damage, although three bombs did land close by and, on one occasion, there was some damage to the church as a result of a nearby bomb explosion. In spring of 1941, the Quarterly Methodist Meeting minutes recorded:

> Acton Hill Church and premises were damaged by blast. The Church and manse roofs and stone masonry suffered considerable damage, also the leaded lights and window frames, etc.[13]

13   Ealing History Centre: Ealing and Acton Circuit, Acton Hill Quarterly Meeting Minutes.

As in the First World War, there was great resolution to help raise money on the home front for the war effort. There were many fund-raising events held in the church at Acton Hill including garden parties and evening entertainment shows which would have also acted as morale boosters for the local people. There was a comprehensive program of salvage drives to remove any surplus which included metals, clothing, paper, etc., although the final metal railings were not taken from outside the church until July 1943.[14]

During the war many inexplicable occurrences happened. One such stressful occasion was a Midnight Baptism at the end of 1941. Herbert described what happened:

> One night in London when the air-raid sirens were wailing, the telephone brought a call from a hospital, some miles away: would I go and baptise a dying baby. I did not know the hospital, nor the sister who made the call; nor the heart-broken mother. The only bus available took me half-way; the rest was a walk through streets as deserted as though the population had already fled. At the hospital I found a sister who worshipped when possible in the Church of which I was minister. We sat down to discuss the exact case of the tiny creature who lay there in his oxygen tent, breathing fitfully. "Could he live?" 'Medically no.'

Herbert was to discover twenty years later of a fine healthy young man who was baptised in such circumstances during the worst days of the Blitz. He discovered that the young man was 'the subject of the midnight sacrament' (as described later by Herbert).

Most of the young children of Acton had been evacuated but some of the older children remained in the area and took on practical roles helping in the war effort, including the Acton Hill Methodist Church's boy scouts being involved with civil defence duties. Herbert could see the need for a youth organisation for those children who were too old for the scouts and perhaps not old enough to sign-up to the services, so in 1941 he set up a successful new group in the church called 'The Good Companions Youth Club'. In October 1942, the church celebrated 21 years of scouting at Acton Hill.[15] Herbert was their minister and also their chaplain. At commemorative services Herbert read out the names of the fifty scouts who were now serving in the forces.[16]

In June 1943, a memorial tablet was unveiled at Acton Methodist Church in memory of 19-year-old Ronald Brown, the first Acton Boy Scout to be killed in action on 23 November 1939. At the service, the Rev. Cowl said:

> Ronald Brown was called to take part in a glorious deed in English history, known to everyone. When he felt the 'Rawalpindi' turn into action choosing

---

14   *Acton Gazette and West London Post*, 16 July 1943.
15   *Acton Gazette and West London Post*, 4 September 1942.
16   Ibid.

to go down with all its guns firing, he could not see and know exactly what was happening. Yet it was a moment in history which will be remembered. In his life, and yours, there is something deeper than we know at the moment. It does not matter whether we live a long time or a little time, so long as we do live.[17]

The war years rolled on and Herbert continued his vital role in helping the local community in and around Acton. Their son Michael was now overseas serving with the Royal Navy facing different challenges and risks on various warships throughout the conflict. Their daughter June continued her work in the Secret Service with nobody knowing or understanding where she was or what she was doing. Uncertain times continued as the war seemed never-ending.

On 22 February 1944, a German bomb struck Twyford Crescent leaving a crater 40 to 50 feet in diameter and some 10 feet deep.[18] Danger was everywhere and anybody at any time could become a victim of the war.

In June 1944, Herbert wrote to one of his dearest friends, the Rev. Derrick Greeves describing the scene on the evening when the Chapel of the Ascension in Bayswater, Central London, was destroyed during a German bombing raid:

> I stood in the Uxbridge Road, outside our Church at Acton Hill, at 3.00 am. I had settled the folk brought in from shattered homes that night; they were sleeping on pews and chancel floor; and all was quiet there. Looking along the road to the East, the sky was scarlet with a sea of leaping flames from some part of London that was ablaze. In the late afternoon of the same day, I stood (despite the traffic!) in the same spot and looked in the same direction. A great thunder cloud stood away to the East and the whole sky that in the early hours had been filled with hell was arched over now with one of the sublimest rainbows I have ever seen.

Concerned for her safety, Herbert sent May down to Hampreston for most of the war. However, despite all the prevailing hardships in London, whenever there was opportunity, Herbert would go down to Dorset to see her, but by the end of 1944, May was convinced that her place was back home in London at Herbert's side.

The lease for Newton Cottage had been signed on 1 December 1939, but it was not until 1945 that Herbert officially took on the tenancy of his new 'Wonderland' on the Isle of Purbeck in its remote colourful location with flora and history in abundance. Permanent residence there would not follow until after his retirement; however he saw this cottage as an opportunity to help his parishioners in need during the later years of the war. There were many families who enjoyed the invitation that was extended to them during these times of hardship. When he could see that members of his

17   *Acton Gazette and West London* Post, 4 June 1943.
18   Ealing History Centre, Borough of Acton, Serious Damage to Property reports.

congregation were suffering with bereavement, illness or exhaustion, he would often offer them the use of Newton Cottage as a free destination for a vacation – a place of peace where his parishioners and friends could rest. This sometimes involved sending a husband and wife down to Dorset whilst he and May entertained their children as guests in the Manse. This also gave the children an insight into the life of their Methodist minister and they learnt to respect how hard he worked and how involved he was with the local community.

Although a much loved minister, it is interesting to note that some of Herbert's parishioners did not take kindly to their minister having the initials 'M.C.' after his name, reminding them that he had been recognised for the role he played in the First World War. This prejudice had its origins in the pacifist tendencies of some Methodists, amongst other denominations, who refused to come to terms with a perceived 'new' concept of military chaplaincy, viewing such service as a sacrilegious travesty of the gospel of peace. Some even chose to move away from the Hendon and Acton Hill Methodist Churches because of their views. Nevertheless, the vast majority felt very honoured to have the Rev. H.B. Cowl M.C. as their minister.

After the war Herbert told one of the school boys at Wycliffe that he had been a 'pacifist' (many years ago), but later became an "ultra-non-pacifist". He told the young man after the service that a member of the congregation had told him how pleased she was to hear a minister say he was a pacifist. Herbert said it was 'frustrating to discover that people understood the exact opposite of what he was saying'.

The war was over. Unlike the end of the Great War where celebrations had erupted with unrestrained joy, the end of the Second World War on 8 May 1945 came to pass with mixed bitter sweet emotions as the country was still at war with Japan, and this war would continue for several more months until August. However, VE (Victory in Europe) Day brought much joy to the people. Hundreds of street parties were organised throughout the area and across all the boroughs of London. In Acton bonfires were lit, streets and houses were decorated and the church bells rang in celebration of peace. Thanksgiving services were held in all the local churches.

For Herbert and May, a deep sense of personal joy must have accompanied the shared relief that Michael and June had survived and they would be coming home.

Despite many members of the church wanting the Rev. Cowl to extend his ministry at Acton Hill, at the end of the war in 1945 Herbert and May moved to their last Methodist circuit in Torquay, where Herbert was to serve the people of the South Devon coast town as their Methodist minister for four years. Hardships continued in the form of rationing but Herbert and May benefitted from food parcels sent to them from May's family in British Columbia which included, on at least one occasion, fresh moose!

However, the memories of the First World War never left him and he was often reminded of some of those vivid recollections that he had experienced during his service as an Army Chaplain.

Whilst at Torquay, on one occasion, Herbert remembered an encounter he had with a visitor passing his church:

A man came to see me whom I had never met before: spending his holiday in Torquay. He saw my name outside the church and it turned out that I had known his brother in the DLI in 1915. He was our first casualty. Great fellow with a fine record in training. When we'd been in line for three nights we brought his body in.

It seemed so futile. And I had to write to his mother. The reason she and her remaining son had remembered ever since was that all four of us knew something else about his death: 'When he died. Everyone Died.'

(He never saw the enemy; he never fired a shot.) Party that helped me bury him were so nearly caught by sudden burst of shell fire, I thought his death would cost us half a dozen more.

At the end of their time in Torquay, Herbert and May were due to retire from ministerial life, but Herbert was drawn back to Wycliffe for one last time. The school had been without a Chaplain for some time as a suitable candidate could not be found. So, the Headmaster, Mr W.A. Sibly at Wycliffe College asked for Herbert to return. By the end of 1949, Herbert and May were back in Stonehouse with Herbert once more taking on the role of School Chaplain. They stayed in Stonehouse for three years until Herbert finally found a suitable replacement. He was now ready to retire. Before leaving the school, Mr Sibly said, 'Never has the school had a more popular Chaplain or one more loved.'

The school journal described the Rev. Cowl as having, 'the experience of years, but retains the heart of a boy'. His departure imminent, the last word in *The Wycliffe Star* read:

> We and many another have gone to him with our troubles; sometimes he answered in parables, but he always breathes wisdom and Christianity. Mr and Mrs Cowl return to their haven of peace in Dorset.[19]

In 1952 Herbert retired and he and May moved to Newton Cottage near Corfe Castle on the Isle of Purbeck, their new permanent home, where he became a Supernumerary[20] minister involved in the local community and preached in the Swanage Methodist Circuit. However, he and May also spent time in Bournemouth at Herbert's late father's house at 24, Eldon Road.

Thirty-five years after meeting May at Foggathorpe, Herbert presented her with a small hymn book. On a card insert he wrote:

> In a Yorkshire Village near Selby town
> A student came preaching without a gown;
> Nor had he a collar or clerical hue
> But O! with what rapture his eye fell on you.

19   *The Wycliffe Star*, March 1952–August 1952.
20   Name given to a retired Methodist Minister.

Now he sees you more lovely than e'er he can say
Tho' it's ... 35 years Ago TO-DAY!

Subsequent years of blissful retirement were spent on the Isle of Purbeck. They were accompanied by their much loved little dog, a Dachshund named Simon (who only ate fresh rabbit).

From an early age, Herbert recalled happy memories of escaping his early school days in London, to discovering the beauty of the Dorset coast, the Isle of Purbeck and the Purbeck hills and cliffs. It was Newton Cottage that was to become Herbert's natural and spiritual home, a peaceful haven of tranquillity – being at one with nature must have seemed heavenly after the years of pastoral service in London during WW2 and his work in the trenches during WW1. Newton Cottage was his paradise, his sanctuary and a place for contemplative meditational prayer. Herbert and May's children, nephews, nieces and future grandchildren would regularly visit Newton for many decades to come in order to spend magic time with Herbert in his kingdom of peace and solitude. The cottage was set in a very remote location; in the early days there was no electricity – paraffin lamps were used to light the house and a coal-fired Rayburn stove was used for all the cooking. In winter, the stove in the kitchen and one open log fire in the lounge kept the whole house warm. They were very much self-sufficient; milk and eggs were collected daily from a neighbouring farm and May prepared, cooked and baked for Herbert and also for family and friends calling at their home – everything was homemade.

Herbert with his grandsons on the estuary at Newton (1968); a lesson in nature, a good story and happy memories! (Author's collection)

Although retired, Herbert continued to take services at many local Methodist churches. It would have been a regular sight for anyone in the area to see the Rev. Herbert Cowl quietly riding around the lanes and tracks on his old motorcycle (an old Enfield or similar). The old bike was warmly referred to as 'Katie Kay' (number plate: KTK 851). He had mastered the springy suspension and was very capable of weaving his way around the holes and puddles on the Goathorn Peninsula. He would often turn up at a local church in the middle of winter on his motorcycle ready to take the service wearing his long trench coat drenched from head to toe!

Herbert returned to Portsmouth and on several occasions preached at Trinity Methodist Church in Albert Road, Southsea. He also had great tolerance and acceptance of other faiths and involved himself with other organisations, including the Quakers and the Salvation Army. He was also a great advocate of the Methodist charity, the National Children's Home.[21] Even as far back as 1917, Herbert had made contributions to the charity and he found great joy in giving to children. During the First World War, the cost of the war in human terms had meant that there were many boys and girls who had become orphaned across the country.

In 1958 on Trafalgar Day, Herbert and May's first grandchild was born exactly 42 years after Herbert was presented with the Military Cross medal by the King at Buckingham Palace.

A second grandson followed in November 1964 and in May 1965, their third and last grandchild was born, a granddaughter.

Such joy was followed by great sadness as May's health started to deteriorate. May had always been a very strong woman – in all ways. She was kind and generous, although true to her upbringing, she did not 'suffer fools gladly' and this often showed with her foreboding presence. After a prolonged period of poor health and bed rest, six months later, Herbert's beloved Maisie, Mary Louise passed away, aged 74.

In the Bournemouth North Cemetery Book of Remembrance the following anecdote was recorded:

> Cowl Mary Louise of Yorkshire; British Columbia; Newton Bay, Poole Harbour. Died 6th December 1965. "The Climate of her nature was a clear, steady sunshine".

As always, faith kept him strong. His marriage to May had been long and very happy.

Herbert went through a difficult time in his life after May's death. Although he understood, he found it difficult to come to terms with her loss. Despite having a caring family he was lonely. His daughter June was married and living overseas and his son Michael was married and farming in Pembrokeshire. He missed May greatly.

---

21   National Children's Home Charity founded by Wesleyan Methodists and in 2008 charity re-named 'Action for Children'.

However, in the ensuing years Herbert started to spend more time with an old family friend from Hendon, an unmarried Beryl Amy Fairminer, a few years younger than Herbert, who had now relocated to Highcliffe-on-Sea near Christchurch in Dorset. Over the coming years their friendship grew as they spent more time together enjoying each other's company, and in October 1970 Herbert and Beryl were married. It was a quiet ceremony held at Highcliffe Methodist Church.

Soon afterwards, Herbert became ill with a rare type of leukaemia. Beryl (who became affectionately known by the family as 'Auntie Beryl') nursed him and gave him comfort and friendship in the last months of his life. However, despite all the diligent care and nursing, Herbert's health continued to decline and he died peacefully on Wednesday 7 July 1971 at Beryl's home, 14B Stuart Road in Highcliffe, aged 85. He and Beryl had been married for less than one year.

At 2.15 pm, on Monday 12 July 1971 Herbert's funeral took place at Victoria Park Methodist Church in Bournemouth.[22] A large group of mourners included family, friends and fellow clergymen attended. Prominent Methodist minister and dearest friend, the Rev. Derrick Greeves spoke of Herbert's life; his retirement to 'Wonderland', 'his painful career as an Army Chaplain' and his 'sixteen years in London' including, 'typically active service among the bombs.' He also spoke of the man – this man so bright and rich in spirit!

> As a minister he was a lesson and a model to us all – a greater influence than he ever knew.
>
> Born into a minister's home, he was always professional but never clerical. He could surely have won an international prize in the gentle art of avoiding committees, consultations, conferences and such like carryings-on! Time and again at a District Synod, you would find him playing truant, bird-watching.
>
> As a pastor – he was so attractive a person that people always wanted more of him than he had time to give. He could never treat people in a superficial way. No nonsense – by love and intuition rather than by technique.
>
> When Herbert Cowl died a great locked safe was dropped to the bottom of the deepest oblivion – with all the secrets men and women had told him.
>
> A sense of wonder – life was one big 'Well I never!' He was a natural Naturalist – not a school-boy collector of things, but a man who kept getting caught up in a bit of God's creation, who was just thrilled to be in on the act.
>
> As for love – we could all of us tell our separate story of his overflowing affection. May and the family were the pride and passion of his life, never diminished.

And, so a large gathering of family, friends and colleagues said their farewells to Herbert.

---

22 *The Bournemouth Times*, 9 July 1971.

Herbert and May in retirement together with their Canadian Duck Punt on the water's edge at Newton Cottage, Poole Harbour. (Author's collection)

A few days later, Herbert's ashes were scattered with May's on the rose beds at North Cemetery in Bournemouth near to the final resting place of Herbert's father, the Rev. Frederick Bond Cowl, who had been buried at the cemetery 34 years earlier. Herbert and May's names were recorded in the cemetery Book of Remembrance.

Underneath the short record of remembrance for the memory of Herbert, there are five words noted:

'A very perfect, gentle knight.'[23]

23   Words taken from Geoffrey Chaucer's medieval classic *The Canterbury Tales* (1478).

The Rev. H.B. Cowl M.C. lived a life with God and his faith at the very centre of his own existence and he once wrote to a friend:

> I'm no mystic. I haven't a shred of the discipline and persistence and consistency that goes with genuine mysticism. But I know Him whom I have believed. It is just stark reality, learned through the desperate struggles of youth, the shatterings of war, the discoveries of human love, and in and through it all – contact with those beloved women and men of God who had found in Him what is now so vital a treasure to me.

NATIONAL MEMORIAL ARBORETUM

Staffordshire

On

21 July 2015

The RAChD Memorial

unveiled as a tribute to all the Chaplains who gave
their lives during the course of their duty

WE SHALL REMEMBER THEM

Ave crux spes unica mea:
Hail to the Cross, my only hope.

Herbert's Roll of Honour

Private JOE FOSTER – Black Watch (Royal Highland Regiment)

Herbert described Joe Foster of the 9th (Scottish) Division, whom he had first met at Bordon Camp as follows:

> He was short and thick-set, but some grey hairs told that he need not have come: he could have stayed in the mine earning good money. It was no popular rush that carried him into the armed forces. There lay his story. It was some weeks before he told it, but one night, when a handful of us sat talking into the small hours, it came out.

Touched by Joe's story, he never forgot him:

> He came like a breath of life to me, at Bordon Camp. He had joined up in order to win over his old drinking pals. He had been a heavy drinker, by which his home was ruined, but three times, he claimed, God spoke to him. One Friday night, as the pub closed, he begged his nearest friend for the money to pay his rent next day, or out went wife and children. His friend took the money from his pocket and said, "Joe, you are a filthy dog, and I wouldn't soil my hands by giving it you." So he tossed it in the mud for Joe to gather up. The lash of that sudden scorn pulled him up for several weeks. Then it all began again. Next time the word came their way; staggering homewards at midnight he fell, & slept where he fell. He woke with daylight, to find himself on the lip of a disused pit shaft, where inches of movement would have plunged him down 300ft. This time reform lasted a few more weeks; and then he broke again. The third call got through to the hidden man of the heart. His old mother came to stay, and on Sunday night begged Joe to stay home and read to her. Angry and ashamed he stayed. She gave him to read one of Spurgeon's sermons. What the text or subject matter, he could never anyhow recall; but that night misery stole his sleep; and at work next day he sought over two quiet, God-fearing men amongst his work mates of whom he had heard, told them of his plight and asked them keep. There in the workshop they prayed with him; and there he gave himself to God. He had horrified me by producing at our 'Men's Free & Easy' in camp, a proof, based

on half-a-dozen texts, that he would come through unscathed. Yet, so he did, for I heard some years later that he was settled in a small shop in a radiant home in Edinburgh.

There were several men by the name of Joe Foster that served as privates in the Black Watch during the First World War. We do not know to which Herbert refers, but we do know he inspired the newly commissioned Army Chaplain.

Dr PHILIP GOSSE – RAMC

Philip Gosse was a doctor billeted with Herbert at Gris Pot in Flanders. Herbert found him a fascinating companion during those latter days at the Advanced Dressing Station near to the front line. He referred to him fondly as 'The Doc.'. Philip Henry George Gosse was the grandson of naturalist Philip Henry Gosse and only son of the poet, author and critic, Sir Edmund William Gosse.

Philip Gosse had his own great interest in small mammals, particularly mice. One day, he found his colleague, Dr Charles McKerrow, skinning a field vole in order to make small hand muffs for his child's doll back home, and it inspired Philip Gosse to write to his friend at the Natural History Museum in London to ask whether the Museum had sufficient specimens of the small mammals to be found in Flanders and, if not, would he like his friend in Flanders to procure some more. So, Philip Gosse set about the task.

Mouse traps were acquired in Armentières and 'The Doc.' began setting traps across the area, in ditches, hedges and in the trenches. He would set them with ration cheese as bait and, to remind himself of where the traps were placed, he put a small piece of cotton wool near the set trap on a twig or bramble. He would then bring back the specimens, examine and measure them. They would be labelled with details on the variety, sex, measurements, etc. The next task was to complete the job of taxidermy. The mouse would be stuffed with army cotton wool, sewn up with needle and thread, pinned onto a board to dry and the final job was to place a label on its off-side hind leg.

Today, there are small animals at the Natural History Museum that were collected in Western Europe during WW1. Dr Philip Gosse's work will be remembered into perpetuity.

Philip Gosse's collection of mice, voles and shrews kept him busy when he was not performing his duties as a medical officer on the front line. Also, Philip Gosse shared Herbert's interest in ornithology and he commented in his book, A Naturalist Goes to War; 'Without the birds I dare not think how I should have gone through the War at all'.

However, during his duty and work in the RAMC, we know from Herbert what a brave man he was and how he turned fear into admirable courage.

Dr Philip Henry George Gosse of the RAMC survived the war. His military service as a doctor took him south to the Somme and Poperinge and on to Khandala, Poona and the Nilgiri Hills in India.

After the war, Philip Gosse became an acclaimed writer and a naturalist following in his famous father's footsteps. He wrote of the Army Chaplain he had known and who was wounded in 1915:

> I missed him very much and missed as well the fresh roses which he used to pick each day in the ruined gardens to decorate our cellar.[1]

Private ALFRED GRIFFITHS – Driver with the Royal Army Service Corps (RASC)

Alfred Griffiths' grave, front row (centre), at Erquinghem-Lys. (Author's collection)

On 9 November 1915 Private Alfred Griffiths, whilst attached to the 69th Field Ambulance / Royal Army Medical Corps, was wounded by German shrapnel when trying to move the motor ambulance out of the shelled buildings at Gris Pot so that the wounded Army Chaplain, Herbert could be saved and taken to the CCS in Bailleul. Alfred died the following day from his injuries – internal wounds, 'wound back

---

1   Philip Gosse, Memoirs of a Camp-follower (London, New York & Toronto: Longmans, Green and Co., 1934).

penetrating lungs' caused by the shrapnel. Private A. Griffiths is buried and remem-bered at the cemetery behind the church, Paroisse Saint Martin, in Erquinghem-Lys.

Alfred was born and bred in Bradford, Yorkshire and was a Master Electrician by trade. He joined the war in June 1915 as a private in a Mechanical Transport battalion in the Army Service Corps.

Alfred was married to Ruth Eliza Seller for ten years. They had no children. When he was lying in a bed at the CCS and near to death, he asked the Army Chaplain at his bedside, the Rev. Wilfred Leveson Henderson (an Anglican Army Chaplain attached to the 69th Brigade), to write to one of his wife's best friends, Miss Faires instead of his wife. This request was made because he wanted his wife Ruth to have her friend with her, when she was to learn of his death. The Rev. Henderson wrote the following:

> I have sad news to give you and a sad duty to ask you to perform. Pte Griffiths of the ASC Motor Transport was seriously wounded yesterday and died to-day at 12.45 pm. Before his death he asked that any news of him might be sent direct to you. He felt that it would be kinder that his wife should hear of his wounds, and as it has happened of his death, from a friend than by a letter from one who is a stranger. Would you let her know how nobly he did his duty? About 2 o'clock yesterday our Advanced Dressing Station came under very heavy shell fire, during which one of the Chaplains was wounded. Pte Alfred Griffiths at great personal risk immediately went to get his ambulance car, and it was while attempting to do this he was hit. I may say that he has been commended for his bravery.[2]

Ruth, overcome by grief, never recovered. Two years later in 1917 she died from what some of her family members said was a broken heart. Her death certificate recorded 'Mitral Regurgitation' – in effect a broken heart!

Dr. CHARLES McKERROW – RAMC

Charles Kenneth McKerrow was a good friend of Herbert and he was billeted with him in France and Flanders. He was a captain with the 68th Brigade and attached to the 10th Battalion of the Northumberland Fusiliers for the duration of his war as a Regimental Medical Officer.

Charles McKerrow was born in Ayrshire in 1883. He was educated at Cargilfield Preparatory School in Edinburgh, Charterhouse School in Kent and Clare College, Cambridge. Before the war he practised medicine with his father, George McKerrow, in Ayrshire.

On 23 January 1915, Charles Kenneth McKerrow married his sweetheart, Jane Beckwith Craik in Galloway. Shortly afterwards, Charles joined the British

2   Musée de la Cité d'Ercan, Erquinghem-Lys.

Expeditionary Force and became part of the 23rd Division and the 68th Brigade. It was at this time that he and Herbert became good friends. They shared many interests including poetry, fishing and astronomy. During those early days in France, close friendships were formed and Herbert often referred to his good friend, 'McKerrow'.

Whilst serving in the northern Pas de Calais, when time and opportunity allowed, McKerrow and Herbert often dined together and on 31 August 1915, McKerrow wrote in his diary of the Padre Cowl; '39 at S.P.[Strongpoint] Too many. Largely sore feet and boils. Breakfast with Q.M.[Quartermaster] and Padre. Too late for the eggs … The padre is a decent fellow …'

On one memorable day, Charles McKerrow was found skinning a field vole so, like his colleague, Dr Philip Gosse, he was fascinated by small creatures.

Captain Charles McKerrow RAMC.
(*The Sphere*)

When not on duty he also spent time intent on ridding his dugout of vermin, which often meant shooting rats with his automatic pistol.

Dr Charles McKerrow soon became a much loved and respected medical officer in the 68th Brigade. He was much cared for by the local people too, who had discovered the doctor billeted in their village. In his spare time, he was soon practising as a GP for some of the local inhabitants and on one occasion he even acted as a veterinary surgeon to help a farmer with his cows who had been wounded with shrapnel.

Whilst in action on 20 December 1916 at Maple Copse, he was badly injured in the course of duty. Dr Philip Gosse visited him that day – they both knew that he would not survive his injuries and Charles McKerrow died later that same day from his inoperable wounds. He was buried before the end of the day in a local village. He was 33 years of age and left a widow and a young son, George Hamilton McKerrow (born two days after the sinking of the Anglia). Captain Charles Kenneth McKerrow is buried and remembered at Lijssenthoek Military Cemetery in Belgium. He is also named and remembered on the Clare College War Memorial in Cambridge and in the Cargilfield Prep School memorial chapel in Scotland.

His wife re-married some years later and sadly his son died aged 7 on 31 May 1922 at the Hospital for Sick Children in York, Toronto in Canada.

Charles McKerrow kept a diary during the war and in it he described on several occasions how he sought the company of Herbert Cowl. Their feeling of friendship must have been very much mutual.

The Rev. SYDNEY JACOBY – Royal Army Chaplain's Department (RAChD), Highland Light Infantry (HLI), King's African Rifles (KAR), Royal Air Force (RAF)

Herbert knew the Rev. Sydney Pearson Jacoby from his early days in the ministry when they were both on probation. However, Sydney Jacoby was born into a Jewish family in Kilburn, London in 1884 and at some point in his youth converted to the Wesleyan Methodist faith. He entered the ministry in 1911. Prior to the war he was a Wesleyan minister in the village of Sawtry in Cambridgeshire. On 8 January 1915[3] Sydney was appointed as a Wesleyan Army Chaplain to the Garrison in Devonport only two weeks after Herbert had signed up to the war effort. Both Herbert's appointment to Bordon Camp and Sydney's appointment to Devonport were announced together at the Wesleyan Army & Naval Committee Meeting in early 1915. Also, both men were involved in the Temperance Committee of the Wesleyan church.[4]

By the autumn of 1915 they were both on their way to the front in Northern France.

Sydney began his war on the northern mainland of France. This is where he and Herbert spent time together, before Herbert moved west towards Flanders and Sydney was sent south to the town of Rouen where he was assigned to the 4th Division Base.

However, after less than a year in his role as an Army Chaplain, it was not long before Sydney Jacoby made the very unusual move of leaving the ministry mid-way through the war. It is not known why he made this decision, although as a peacemaker and Christian, it would have been an extremely difficult and yet brave decision to make!

On 15 March 1916 he relinquished his commission as an Army Chaplain and joined the Highland Light Infantry as a combatant in France with the rank of Second Lieutenant.[5] His enrolment to the HLI was announced less than two weeks later in The London Gazette.[6] His new role was described as 'temporary' and that he was 'on probation'. At a meeting of the Wesleyan Army and Navy Board on 29 May 1916, the following minute was recorded:

> The board regrets that steps were taken by the Rev. S.P. Jacoby to secure a combatant commission, without previous communication with the Board.

Whilst serving with the HLI Sydney was awarded the Croix de Guerre for his gallant actions.[7]

3   *Birmingham Daily Post*, 15 February 1915.
4   MARC, Wesleyan Methodist Conference Minutes, 1915.
5   *The London Gazette*, 26 March 1916.
6   Ibid., 28 March 1916
7   *The Methodist Recorder*, 22 November 1917

However, he was soon to be seconded to the Colonial service with The King's African Rifles in German East Africa (now known as Tanzania) on a 'temporary commission' as a Lieutenant. In 1917 Wesleyan Methodist Records described his deployment with 'eight months bush fighting'. He spent time in Durban in the Natal Province and described life in Kilwa:

> It is a country of big game, much sickness, and occasional hard fighting. Machine-guns and bombs play a big part in the War for the Germans' Askaris, native soldiers who are very good fighters and brave men.

At the end of 1918 Sydney (whose name was sometimes spelt Sidney) was finally appointed to the Royal Air Force (previously known as the Royal Flying Corps) as a Lieutenant and Adjutant. He joined the 61st Squadron (which had been created earlier in the war in 1917) flying first Sopwith Pups, followed by Sopwith Camels. He stayed with the 61st Squadron until the end of the war.

In 1919 Sydney was awarded the Military Cross for his Services in East Africa. During his war he had been wounded, experienced life being detained by the enemy, he had contracted Malaria and he had survived!

Sydney Jacoby left the RAF at the end of 1919 and returned to the Wesleyan Church, renewing his faith and vocation to return to a life as a minister. His first circuit after the war was in Manchester where he stayed for a year before moving to St Leonards, East Sussex.

After many years practising as a Methodist minister, the Rev. Sydney Jacoby died in Croydon, Surrey on 29 May 1944 aged 60.

The Rev. ARTHUR FARRINGTON – Royal Army Chaplain's Department (RAChD)

In one of the letters home to his parents in September 1915 from an unknown village in France, Herbert wrote of his excitement at finding some soldiers of the York and Lancaster Regiment and hoped he might find an old friend:

> I dashed off into the town, as I had seen in marching thro' a 'Y & L' man – the Battalion to which dear old Farrington is attached. After an hour or so of hunting I found him, to our mutual unfeigned delight!

Arthur Farrington was born in London in 1871, the eldest son of a boot maker and he started his working life as a clerk in the commercial world. However, eventually he was able to follow his true calling in life. He became a local preacher for a Methodist Church, but by 1900 he had decided to join the Congregational Church. At the mature age of 40 he was a married man, a father with three children and the Congregational minister for Southwick Congregational Church in Sunderland. It was during his next ministry in Devon, when in June 1915 he signed up as a Temporary Army Chaplain to the Forces 4th Class. Before he left his church in Okehampton, his congregation thanked him for his 'good work' and described him as having a 'breezy and brotherly nature'. Arthur and Herbert's war began at Bordon Camp, although Arthur had already visited France in 1914 when he had been asked on behalf of the National Brotherhood Council to take and distribute a large assignment of clothing, food and money to the suffering Belgian refugees who had fled their country.

Herbert and Arthur were both assigned to the 23rd Division. Arthur became Chaplain to the Forces to the 70th Infantry Brigade. In fact it was Arthur Farrington CF who signed and witnessed the paperwork at Bordon outlining the terms of Herbert's engagement as an Army Chaplain during the war.

On 27 August 1915, Arthur arrived in France – two days after Herbert. Arthur was stationed with the 9th York

Congregational Church Army Chaplain, the Rev. Arthur Farrington. (Author's collection)

and Lancaster Battalion in the north of the country and he and Herbert met up when they could. We know from Herbert's letters that he even managed to see his old friend take Morning Service on a couple of occasions which must have been a reassuring for Herbert in terms of finding a familiar and dear friend in such near proximity. Like Herbert (and many of the Army Chaplains), Arthur eventually found himself attached to one of the Field Ambulances where he continued to carry out his duties. At some point after 1915, he was re-assigned to the 8th Division. During his time in France, besides carrying out his duties as an Army Chaplain, he organised a Brigade canteen, a Brigade bank, as well as concerts for the troops.

During and after the war, Arthur spoke openly of his views on peace and was often quoted:

> ... at the end of the war he pleaded that instead of a spirit of revenge, a spirit of sacrifice and forgiveness should aid them towards the reconstruction of Europe.

In July 1919, the London Gazette reported in the Gallantry Awards listing that the Rev. Arthur Farrington had been 'Mentioned in Despatches' for 'gallant and distinguished services in the field'.

After the war, Arthur returned to his wife and children in Okehampton, and continued his work as a pastor for the Congregational Church together with his many other favourite causes including the Federation of the National Brotherhood Council.

In 1922 Arthur was offered and accepted a new role at the Birmingham Mission. In the latter years of his life, he became a great champion for the British Legion.

Rev. Arthur Farrington died at his home in Birmingham on 13 February 1955 aged 84.

Nursing Sister MARY RODWELL – Queen Alexandra's Imperial Military Nursing Service (QAIMNS)

One member of the nursing staff died on HMHS Anglia. As Herbert described so grimly in one of his written accounts of what happened on 17 November 1915, we know that the Sister attending to him a moment before the explosion would have been Nursing Sister, Mary Rodwell.

Mary Ann Rodwell was born in Oakley, Suffolk on 7 June 1876, the daughter of a farmer. She trained at Hendon Infirmary Hospital in north-west London from 1901 to 1904. She later nursed at the Samaritan Free Hospital, Marylebone Road, London and before the war she was working in private nursing homes in the capital.[8] Feeling it was her duty to volunteer she joined the QAIMNS, working first on hospital trains before assignment to HMHS *Anglia*.[9] Mary was amongst the nursing staff who attended to King George V on his return from France in October 1915 when he had been injured in a riding accident.

Nurse Mary Rodwell.
(Author's collection)

In a correspondence dated 8 September of that year she wrote:

> The large hospital ships have gone to the Dardanelles leaving us only the small ones for France. I saw the XXXXX she takes 3000 patients and is enormous. I prefer a smaller boat myself, in case anything should go wrong, and just now the German mines are a great many over here. We have also seen (German) submarines at times ... So far we have been lucky with the hospital ships.

---

8   *The British Journal of Nursing*, 11 December 1915.
9   Ibid.

Mary Rodwell was also an enthusiastic suffragette being a supporter of the Crystal Palace and Anerley Women's Freedom League (WFL).

The Matron of Hendon Infirmary wrote to The British Journal of Nursing regarding Nurse Rodwell:

> She herself could wish for no better end than to die with the patients under her care. We all know what a keen sense of duty she possessed. Nothing was ever a trouble to her where her patients were concerned, and she was kind, firm and sympathetic to a degree. She gave all she could at all times to help and comfort those in trouble and need.

Mary Rodwell's next of kin was her father, John Rodwell, who was living at Strawlands in Plumpton, East Sussex.[10] Mary left no will, her pay, washing allowance and gratuity, et al totalling £9 16s 3d were paid directly to her father.

Mary Rodwell is remembered on seven memorials: Hollybrook Memorial in Southampton; the QAIMNS 'Five Sisters' memorial in York Minster; the memorial board in St Paul's Anerley near Penge; Ditchingham parish church on the Norfolk/Suffolk border; at All Saints church in Plumpton Green near Lewes, Sussex; at the former Colindale Hospital, London (closed in 1996) and most recently on a plaque honouring 500 nurses who lost their lives during the First World War at Edinburgh Central Library.

Second Lieutenant ROWLAND GILL M.M. M.C. – King's Liverpool Regiment

Rowland was born in Willington, County Durham in 1884, the second son of Wesleyan Minister, the Rev. Daniel Gill. Rowland attended Kingswood School in Somerset which was often a place where Wesleyan Ministers would send their children for education, although this was not the case for Herbert. Rowland enjoyed school life; participating in the Literary Association, a member of the school cricket team, a prefect, a member of the Reading Room Committee and taking part in school plays. In 1901 he won the prestigious Dix Prize for good conduct.

Following his time at Kingswood, Rowland moved to Headingley College in Leeds where he began his theological studies to become a Wesleyan Minister. Although Raymond Gill was two years older than Herbert, it was at Headingley where they became good friends. In 1908 Raymond Gill was ordained into the Wesleyan Church.

At the beginning of 1914 the Rev. Rowland Gill was the Wesleyan Methodist Minister for Aigburth Vale Church in Liverpool. When war broke out, for some unknown reason, Rowland did not take the path that one would have expected of him

10   TNA WO 399/7168.

in terms of him becoming a Chaplain to the Forces. In September 1914, *The Yorkshire and Leeds Intelligencer* reported:

> The Rev. Rowland Gill, the newly appointed Wesleyan minister at Kilham, near Driffield [West Yorkshire], has informed the Society Stewards that he feels that it is his duty to respond to the country's call, and has offered his services to the nation, which have been accepted.[11]

Rowland Gill enlisted on 31 August 1914 and became possibly one of the first Wesleyan Ministers to join the ranks.

Whilst with the Royal Army Medical Corps in 1916 serving as an orderly with the 43rd Field Ambulance,

The Rev. Rowland Gill, student at Headingley College with Herbert. (Richard Daglish)

in the 14th Division, attached to 42 Brigade, he was awarded the Military Medal for devotion to duty.[12] For five days he had assisted in evacuating wounded from between the front lines under heavy fire at the Somme. In 1917 he became a commissioned officer and was promoted to the position of Temporary Second Lieutenant in the 17th Battalion of The King's Liverpool Regiment.

At the beginning of 1918, Rowland Gill was awarded the Military Cross. *The London Gazette* gave details of his citation:

> For conspicuous gallantry and devotion to duty. Although wounded, he refused medical assistance, and led two platoons forward under machine -gun and shell fire. Later in the day, during heavy shelling of the front line, he walked from post to post across the open, encouraging and cheering the men, and when all the officers of his company had become casualties he took over command, and continued to command with exceptional skill and energy.[13]

---

11   *The Yorkshire and Leeds Intelligencer*, 4 September 1914.
12   *The London Gazette*, 21 December 1916.
13   Ibid.

On 19 April, during the Battle of the Lys, Rowland was reported 'killed in action'. Prior to his death during the chaos of the fighting, Rowland had been reported wounded and then missing. The 17th King's Liverpool Regiment war diarist noted:

> Patrolling was vigorous – 2 Lt R Gill MC MM proceeded on patrol with 5 other ranks – and enemy party was met, shots were exchanged + 2Lt Gill was hit in the head and fell into a ditch, the remainder of the party returned at 4.10 am to our lines.'

On that day, Rowland's Company Commander was Eric Rigby-Jones. At the time of Rowland's disappearance at St. Jans-Cappel (just north-west of Bailleul), it was not known whether he had been killed or not. Eric and his parents were good friends with Rowland. Later in the month, Eric wrote home to his parents:

> This is all I know about Gill. He was ordered on the afternoon of 20 April [war diary details 19 April] to take out a patrol and go up a narrow country lane which led from our lines to a farm-house where there was known to be an enemy post and which he was, if possible, to capture. He took a sergeant and four men and started off at dusk in a diamond formation, he being in the centre. When near the farm the leading man came back and reported a strong party of enemy ahead. Then about twenty Germans rushed out and a bit of a scrap ensued. Gill was shot and rolled into the ditch and our men were driven back. These men got away wounded but Gill was taken in for no sign of him could be seen when we visited the place later in the night. He was undoubtedly badly wounded but there is a good chance of his being safe.

His body was never found and he is remembered on the Tyne Cot Memorial to the Missing. The memorial bears the names of nearly 35,000 officers and men who have no known graves. The Wesleyan Methodist Conference Minutes recorded a moving obituary:

> Everyone knew he was a Wesleyan Minister. As modest as good, he united in the person the consecration of the saint, the culture of the scholar, and the courage of the soldier.[14]

Five of Herbert's fellow theology students from Headingley College gave their lives for the fight for freedom and righteousness in The Great War: Walter Charles Wilks M.C.; Rowland Gill M.M. M.C.; Ernest Wilfred Havelock; Henry Hall Norton M.A. and Sydney Rangeley Hewitt, O.B.E. M.C.

14   Wesleyan Methodist Conference Minutes 1918.

A stained glass window in the chapel at Headingley College (now renamed Hinsley Hall and owned by the Catholic Diocese of Leeds) is dedicated to: 'THE GLORY OF GOD and in grateful memory of these past students of this college who laid down their lives in The Great War 1914 – 1918'. Under the men's names on the plaque are the words: 'Dominus Robur Meum' – the lord is my strength.

The Rev. WILFRID JOHN HARDING M.C. – RAMC & Royal Army Chaplains' Department (RAChD)

Herbert's grandmother, Mary Yeoman Harding descended from the long established Harding family line in Somerset. One of her great nephews, the Rev. Wilfrid John Harding, had been ordained in 1912 after completing his education at Christ's College, Cambridge. At the outbreak of the Great War, he was the curate at Luddenden, a small village near Halifax in Yorkshire.

In 1914 he was eager to sign up to the war effort and on 5 Oct 1914 he was interviewed by the Rt Rev. John Taylor Smith who was the Chaplain-General to the Forces. Unfortunately for Wilfrid he was refused a position as a Chaplain to the Forces on the grounds of lack of experience (despite having two years of experience as

The Rev. Wilfrid John Harding M.C.
(De Ruvignys Roll of Honour)

a curate and being the same age as Herbert) and also that he could not preach without using his notes. So, in order not to be left behind, the Rev. Wilfrid John Harding volunteered and signed up as a private in the Royal Army Medical Corps.[15] He carried out his duties as a stretcher-bearer serving in France and mainly in Boulogne at a Base Hospital. When he had the opportunity, he assisted the Church of England Chaplain stationed in Boulogne and this experience was to serve him well in terms of his second application to become an Army Chaplain in 1917. He never forgot his desire to serve as a Chaplain to the Forces and to serve at the front, so whilst on leave on 4 May 1917 he was interviewed for a second time at the War Office, but this time by the Assistant Chaplain General, the Rev. Canon E.H. Pearce. On this occasion he was successful and before returning overseas, he was able to marry his fiancé, Mary Riley at Lytham St Annes in Lancashire. Two weeks later Wilfrid was a Commissioned Chaplain and on his way back to the front. He left England on 29 May 1917 as Temporary Chaplain

15 *De Ruvignys Roll of Honour.*

to the Forces, 4th Class, Wilfrid was attached to Drake Battalion, 63rd (Royal Naval) Division.

Five months later, on 31 October 1917, Wilfrid was killed during the closing stages of the Third Battle of Ypres or what is still popularly known as 'Passchendaele'. The Drake Battalion's commander wrote to his widow:

> The work for which your husband was awarded the M.C. was as follows: Stretcher-bearers had each case to carry over two miles over the most impossible ground before reaching a road or ambulance. Your husband insisted on going out into "No Man's Land" with the stretcher-bearers in search of wounded men, under the most intense fire and in broad daylight, when he was exposed without cover of any kind, regardless of his own safety so long as he could be a comfort or of use to any of the wounded.[16]

Wilfrid John's citation read: 'For conspicuous gallantry and devotion to duty. He continually attended to the wounded during four days' operations and repeatedly crossed "No Man's Land" under heavy fire to bring them in to the front line.' He is remembered on the Tyne Cot Memorial Panel 160, the Aldershot Memorial in Hampshire and at Christ's College, Cambridge.

16   *St. Anne's Express*, 8 February 1918.

Acknowledgements

There are many people to thank for helping me discover the story of the Army Chaplain, my grandfather, the Rev. Herbert Cowl.

The writing of this book was inspired by a very dear friend, Marion Warnes Bell, one of the most beautiful and unassuming friends anybody could have the pleasure of having in their lives. Without her support, enthusiasm and confidence in me, this story would never have been told. Sadly she has now left this world but her memory will live on in those who had the privilege of having her influence their lives.

Thanks go to my mother, June Mary Cowl, for being the most recent guardian of Herbert's papers, writings and photographs and for her encouragement and relentless pushing for me to complete my grandfather's story.

Although one hundred years have passed since Herbert went to France with the British Expeditionary Force, my special thanks must go to those who have been able to share their personal memories of him with me. These include; Nancy Greeves (wife of the late Rev. Derrick Greeves), the Cowl family, the Trehane family, the Rev. Helen Gardner, John & Nancy Cook, Stephen Pomeroy, Judy Greeves, Stephen Savery, K. Roger Wood, Rosemary Phillips, Tom Norgate, Peter Ford, the Rev. G. Ian Yates, the Rev. Christopher Bamber and Pamela Humphrys.

To those who shared the knowledge of their chosen specialist areas and who helped me understand my grandfather's world during the Great War, I would like to give thanks to: the many Methodist ministers in the Church countrywide who have assisted me in finding information on my grandfather's past life in the church; to The Wesleyan Historical Society for enlightening me on the changing world of the Wesleyan and Methodist Church; to the Rev. Dr Peter Howson, author of *Muddling Through*, for his sound information on Army Chaplaincy; to Peter Forsaith at Oxford Brookes University for his support and access to the archives; to David Blake at the Museum of Army Chaplaincy in Hampshire for his practical understanding of the subject; to John Sheen, author of *With Bayonets Fixed* who gave me strong encouragement in my early days as an author writing about the DLI; to Peter Nelson of the Durham Light Infantry Museum Friends for help on matters relating to the DLI; to Emily Mayhew, author of *Wounded* for sharing her knowledge regarding the relationship between the medics and the padres; to Philip Thornborow, Liaison Officer for Methodist Archives and Peter Knockles at the Manchester Wesley Research Centre at The John Rylands Library for assisting me with my research enquiries.

Huge thanks go to the following who gave me valuable encouragement to write this story; Sue Jackson and Terry Hurst of The North East Methodist History Society and Norma Virgoe for her guidance, time and patience.

Research assistance has been greatly appreciated from the following; Lena Rodgers (Workers Educational Association (WEA) volunteer), Lorraine Coughlan (John Rylands Library), Catherine Roberts (Wycliffe College), Emma Blowers (Local Studies Historian for Hertford Grammar School), Mark Woods (The Methodist Recorder), Jack Thorpe (Curator of Musée de la Cité d'Ercan, Erquinghem-Lys Museum), Liz Topliss (Pastoral Secretary at Sutton Coldfield Methodist Church), John Leake (author of Foggathorpe, A History of Village Life), Shirley Dicker and Vicki Walker (Stonehouse History Group) and thanks to Alexander Poole of Poole's Family Research for copying records at The National Archives.

Lastly but not least, of course to my grandfather – thanks to my wonderful and beautiful Grandad, *The Half-Shilling Curate* Herbert.

Fond Memories

One hundred years have passed since the beginning of the Great War. These are some of the varied memories and recollections from some of the people who have remembered Herbert:

> I recalled with gratitude the outstanding impression your Grandfather made on me when I first arrived at Wycliffe in March 1950 as boy of 13. I had travelled from my home in Sussex by train to the old Stonehouse railway station which was around one mile away from the College. I was met by the Rev. Cowl with his bicycle, sporting a very large basket on the handlebars. Inviting me to place my small suitcase in his basket, he proceeded to escort me, pushing his bike (and my suitcase) all the way to the school. I was making a lone visit to Wycliffe in order to sit my Common Entrance exams which involved me staying a night or two at the school. Your Grandfather was the comforting face of Wycliffe on that first occasion and I have never forgotten his kindness in making me welcome. I have always carried memories of the Rev. Cowl as a gentle man with a hugely impressive voice who went out of his way to make a small boy less desolate than he otherwise would have been.
>
> I duly went to Wycliffe as a pupil during the summer term of 1950 and over the next two years he never failed to acknowledge me with a warm smile whenever our paths crossed. This is something I have never forgotten.
>
> *Stephen, a thirteen-year-old Wycliffe schoolboy (from 1950-1952)*

> I was only 6 when the war started.
>
> My father had taken up the post of organist at Acton Hill Methodist Church. He told me that during his first service that he took, an air raid warning sounded the 'all clear' instead of the 'warning'. Herbert Cowl was most reassuring to the congregation and it was the first time I was aware of his calm and lovely presence.
>
> My own memories of him are very unspecific but he has always stood out for me as a person who was utterly Christian. Whenever I have doubts about my faith the memory of Herbert makes it real for me again. The actual experience of knowing him, seeing him, hearing him talk with his quiet husky voice (he had been wounded in the throat in the 1914-18 war) and enjoying his presence, is, and always has been, a reason for me being a Christian.

I remember him vividly talking to the Sunday School and telling us a story about someone who could not sleep and was wrestling with his bed clothes. For some odd reason I have this mental picture of his laughing face as he spoke of him pulling the sheets so his toes popped out. But the memory of his face is permanently in my mind. It shone with merriment.

My father organised choir parties at our home and I remember sitting by Herbert Cowl on our window seat and enjoying being by him.

It really is extraordinary that his memory has had so much effect on me from so long ago and with such fragmentary actual tangible events to remember. He was a superb human being whose personality shone with love, kindness and humour. I know that my father too admired him and spoke of him as a saint.

I am delighted and warmed by this unexpected contact with you that has made me relive these tiny but vital memories of him. My life as a Methodist minister, a social worker and now retired and involved with our meditation group and local parish Church (I sing in the choir) continues on as a not very good Christian whose times of questioning are answered, not by any mental ponderings but in part by the living memories of someone who is the answer to any doubts – Herbert Cowl.

Christopher, retired Methodist minister from Acton, North London

You never forgot an encounter with Herbert Cowl. We never knew anything about his Military Cross – he would never say a thing about it. My parents idolised him – they worshipped the ground he walked on. The Rev. Cowl was the most under-rated and un-recognised Methodist minister of his time.

In 1933, as minister of Middle Lane Methodist Church in the Highgate Circuit, Herbert Cowl officiated at the marriage of my parents. That is a simple statement of fact but one that conceals a series of relationships – compassionate ministry, friendship, admiration, gratitude and love.

War intervened and in 1945 my father was diagnosed with T.B. and died in 1950 aged 45, leaving my mother with three children and a precarious income. I do not think it an exaggeration to say that Herbert Cowl was a lifeline.

In 1959 I became engaged to a Methodist Minister and went over to meet the Cowls. What an experience! – a table groaning with home baked cooking and a boat trip around Brownsea Island with Herbert rowing, totally alive and responding to every rustle in the reeds, shimmer in the water and birdsong conversations. To say the day was an education would be a gross simplification. I saw the high esteem and enormous gratitude which mother had for the Cowls, both May and Herbert.

Now, after my being a 'minister's wife' for over 50 years I reflect on what is largely a by-gone age which in so many ways has left us the poorer. It seems to me that Herbert Cowl was totally motivated by his faith and belief in God and from that emanated a deep love for his fellow human beings where ever and in whatever circumstances their paths crossed his. Hence he could totally disregard his own safety on a boat in the Channel in wartime and in the warp and woof of everyday life and sadnesses he could pick up our family and show his care in the most practical of ways. I know now we were one of a set of people among many others. Over 60 years on I feel honoured to pay tribute to this giant of a human being, a man largely unsung in Methodist Church circles but so totally loved, valued and remembered down the years as a superlative man of God.

Nancy, retired Methodist minister's wife, Newcastle upon Tyne

I remember him with great affection and respect. He was at Hendon in N.W. London when I was born. He baptised me and he must have stayed there for several years as he looked after me in the church when I was a small boy. He was a lovely gentle caring man. I can still remember his lovely, soft voice different from everyone else's. I just loved listening to this wonderful man.

Roger, a young boy in the 1940's in Hendon, North London

If only we could have this wonderful man with us forever! He radiates an amazing, quiet gentle love and is a true saint … We are so sorry he is leaving tomorrow …

Diary entry for Judy, a 14-year-old schoolgirl, Chelsea, London (1963)

I moved to Swanage, Dorset, aged 7 in April 1954. One of my early memories was hearing your grandfather preach. His passion stuck in my mind, even if his sermons probably meant little to me! My mother and father became great friends with him and your grandmother.

One final memory; one picture which sticks in my mind is your grandfather on his motorcycle, wearing a suitably heavy coat, soaking wet, arriving at Swanage Methodist Church to conduct Morning Service. Water dripping off his glasses and sometimes shivering wet. This was on more than one occasion. The first part of his journey from Newton Cottage on the Goathorn Peninsular to Rempstone; where the roads were made up, must have been extremely unpleasant! I cannot imagine many Methodist ministers travelling by motor cycle these days. I think it summed up his indomitable spirit and in particular the effect of his WWI experiences.

Tom, now retired, previously living in Swanage, Dorset (1954)

He was an unforgettable man. From the pulpit his sermons were compellingly eloquent, graced by the sheer beauty of poetry, typifying the sincere simplicity of one who walked with God in his daily life. His whole being was vibrant with his inner conviction; the bright blue eyes, the suntanned complexion, all spoke of the outdoor man, the man's man. And his voice – who can forget his voice – with its husky diction, the result of war wounds, which compelled added attraction from his hearers, and imparted an even greater significance to his words!

He loved Nature, he loved man – and above all, he loved his God, in whom nature and man were fulfilled and reconciled.

David, retired Wycliffe College Housemaster

He was a great leader of young people. He gave us a good grounding in the New Testament. He was so very kind and so gentle with his intriguing voice. He was such a good teacher – I was thrilled to have had him teach us. He taught us very well.

Sheila, Religious Studies pupil, Torquay (1946)

As a 16-year-old schoolboy carrying out research for a school project, I remember one weekend taking the ferry across Poole Harbour and riding my bike down the rough track towards Newton Cottage in search of the 'Lost Borough' (the ruins of a settlement dating back to the time of King Edward III). I will never forget the warm welcome that I was given by the Rev. Cowl. He was charming and welcoming. I was shown the ruins (which I would have never found without him) and I was invited in for afternoon tea. I was struck by the remoteness of their cottage. I enjoyed a most memorable and unforgettable day with the Rev. Cowl. 60 years on and he has still made an impression on me.

Peter, geology student in the 1960's, Kingswood School, Bath

One evening we were in the garden at dusk and Uncle Herbert stopped what he was doing, put his hand to his ear and told me to listen. I could hear a sort of barking/roaring noise in the woods. He told me that the red deer stags were 'rutting'. Their mating season had started. He knew every inch of the woods, where the clearings were and where the stags would stand and shout their challenges to potential competitors. Next evening we would leave Simon [his dog] in the cottage and creep into the woods to witness this happening.

As dusk fell we were ready and as we heard the first calls from a stag in the nearby woods near a clearing, we crept quietly into the woods, taking care not to snap twigs underfoot, heading towards its margin from a 'down-wind' direction so any stag wouldn't pick up our scent, and hid behind a big tree. No sign of a stag. Uncle Herbert told me to stay very still and to keep well hidden. Then he started to mimic the challenging sound of a rutting deer, primitive and eerily echoing in the forest as he repeated it several times. Within minutes a large red stag came charging into the clearing, head up, nostrils flaring, ready for battle.

Uncle Herbert was soon beside me hiding behind the tree, watching as the stag pawed the ground and roared his own challenge, head up, neck stretched to show off his magnificent antlers. A truly awe-inspiring, fearful sight. Unanswered now as Herbert had decided that discretion was the better part of valour and he was no longer a stag. On that occasion a real challenger did not appear, so we waited until our stag calmed down and put his head down to graze. Danger over. When Uncle Herbert deemed it safe we made our way quietly back to Newton Cottage where Auntie May was waiting for us to join her for a night-time cup of hot chocolate.

Apart from the drama of this event it was Uncle Herbert's deep knowledge and love of the history of the peninsula, its woods and wildlife, his own quiet humanity and understanding of all living things that made such a lasting impression on me. Above all was his ability to convey love, peace and wisdom.

Jennifer, great niece and regular childhood visitor to Newton Cottage

When I was sent reluctantly at seven weeks' notice to Westminster Central Hall, Herbert knew that I would be a scared rabbit. He prayed himself into my situation; he came and left, unseen by me, to the first evening service. 'I looked', he wrote later, 'for one thing, to see if the preacher halted for a moment as he entered the pulpit in order that the Master of the House might precede him'. From then on he kept 'a special tryst' for me, as he did for so many others.

Herbert Cowl became known as my 'Father in God'.

The late Rev. Derrick Greeves, Superintendent Minister, Westminster Central Hall, London (1964)

… he would greet me with a sweeping bow and 'Ah, Princess Juliana Vere de Vere!', which puzzled me a bit, but made me feel special.

A young child's memory

One morning he received a letter addressed to him as Captain the Reverend H Cowl MC. With a wry smile he commented that the sender never addressed him without his military rank, in contrast to some who had written to him in the 1930s criticising him for his decoration on the grounds that it was a wicked thing for a Methodist Minister to receive awards for killing people. Little did they know, he said, that he had received the medal for saving lives, not for killing. And then he told me of the events on the ill fated hospital ship, and of his prayer at the bottom of the sea.

He [Herbert] commented that his wife had died six years previously, and then a pause, 'Or was it yesterday?'

Ian, a retired Methodist Minister who had known Rev. Cowl in Bournemouth (c.1970)

He was my guiding light and if he knew now how many times I have let him down in my life I know his response would be compassion, not condemnation. That was the man and I still love him dearly.

A not so young child's memory

And a final word from Herbert ...

There is all the room in the world for the young and that's right, but there is very little for the very old. Don't be scornful when we old turn away from the noisy crowded days to the still point of the turning world, into a world other than that of time and space.

Rev. Herbert Butler Cowl, M.C.

Bibliography

Author's collection

The private and unpublished letters/writings of the Rev. Herbert Butler Cowl M.C.

Museums & Archives

Barnet Local Studies and Archives, Hendon Library
Bristol Archives
    Bristol Records Office: Clifton Circuit, Bristol Quarterly Meeting Minutes
    Bristol Records Office: NRA 17791 Clifton Circuit, Accs 32397, 37979
Durham Light Infantry Museum
Durham Record Office
Ealing Local History Centre
Fusiliers Museum of Northumberland, Alnwick
Holyhead Maritime Museum
Imperial War Museum, London
John Rylands Library, Manchester: Methodist Archives and Research Centre
    Courtesy of the University of Manchester and the Trustees for Methodist Church Purposes.
    MARC, Minutes Armed Forces Board, 1911 – 1925
    MARC, Minutes of Bordon Soldiers' Home Committee of Management & Trustees Meetings, Sept. 1904 to Dec. 1938
    MARC, Bristol and Bath District Minute Book 1912 – 1914
    MARC, Portsmouth District Minutes
    MARC, Wesleyan Methodist Conference, Agendas
    MARC, Wesleyan Methodist Conference, Minutes
Museum of Army Chaplaincy, Amport, Hampshire
National Army Museum
Oxford Brookes University
Portsmouth History Centre
The National Archives, Kew (TNA) War Office Papers
    WO 95/2181/1: 68th Brigade War Diary

WO 95/2167/1: 23rd Division Headquarters Branches and Services, General Staff
WO 95/2182/2: 13th Battalion DLI Adjutant's War Diary
WO 95/2182/1: 12th Battalion DLI War Diary
WO 95/2182/4: 11th Battalion DLI War Diary
WO 95/2182/3: 10th Battalion NF War Diary
WO 95/2179/1: 69th Field Ambulance War Diary
WO 95/2179/3: 71st Field Ambulance War Diary
WO 95/342/1: 8th Casualty Clearing Station
WO 95/4142/1: Lines of Communication Troops. Hospital Ship, Anglia
WO 339/47342: Service Record of H.B. Cowl
WO 399/7168: Service Record for M. Rodwell
AIR 76/252/129: Service Record for Sidney Pearson Jacoby
ADM 1/8443/367: Admiralty report on the sinking of HMHS *Anglia*

Periodicals and Journals

Army Lists 1914-1918, Army Chaplains Department WW1
British Journal of Nursing
Journal of the Royal Army Chaplains' Department
St George's Gazette
The Hertfordian
The Methodist Recorder
The Methodist Times
The Lady's World
The London Gazette
The Record
The Sphere
The Wesley Historical Society
The Windsor Magazine
The Wycliffe Star

Newspapers

Aberdeen Evening Express
Acton Gazette and West London Post
Birmingham Daily Post
Birmingham Gazette
The Bournemouth Times
The Daily Mail
Gloucester Citizen
New York Times
Oldham Chronicle

Portsmouth Evening News
The Selby Times and Howdenshire and Goole Advertiser
Somerset and West of England Advertiser
The Sunday Times
The Sutton Coldfield News
The Toronto World
St Annes Express
The Times
Western Daily Press
The Western Mail
Yorkshire Post and Leeds Intelligencer
L'echo de la Presse
Le Figaro
Le Gaulois
Le Matin

Books

The Rev. Sir Genille Cave-Browne-Cave Bart., *From Cowboy to Pulpit* (London: Herbert Jenkins Limited, 1926).

Maureen Colledge, *Tin hats doodlebugs & food rations* (London: Acton History Group, 2014).

Philip Gosse, *Memoirs of a Camp-follower* (London, New York & Toronto: Longmans, Green and Co., 1934).

Peter Howson, *Muddling Through* (Solihull: Helion & Company Limited, 2013).

Emily Mayhew, *Wounded* (London: The Bodley Head, 2013).

Stephen McGreal, *The War on Hospital Ships 1914–1918* (Barnsley: Pen & Sword 2008).

Captain Wilfrid Miles, *The Durham Forces in the Field 1914–1918* (London: Cassell, 1920).

Lieut-colonel H.R. Sandilands, *The 23rd Division 1914–1919* (Edinburgh and London: William Blackwood & Sons, 1925).

John Sheen, *With Bayonets Fixed* (Barnsley: Pen & Sword, 2013).

Melvin Charles Smith, *Awarded for Valour: A History of the Victoria Cross and the Evolution of British Heroism* (Basingstoke: Palgrave Macmillan, 2008).

Michael Snape, *God and the British Soldier* (London: Routledge, 2005).

Frederic C. Spurr, *Some Chaplains in Khaki* (London: H.R. Allenson Ltd. and The Kingsgate Press, 1915).

The Army and Religion: An Enquiry and its Bearing upon the Religious Life of the Nation (London: Macmillan and Co. Limited, 1919).

Mrs Arthur Walters, *My Wayside* (London: The Epworth Press, 1930).

W.A.S. and J.D.N, *Wycliffe and the War* (Gloucester: John Bellows, 1923).

Who's Who in Methodism (London: The Methodist Times and Leader, 1933).

Other works cited in text

De Ruvignys Roll of Honour
The Scout Association – Official Handbook (1910)
Various circuit papers (including Bristol, Bournemouth, Ealing, Hendon and Swanage)

Electronic Sources

www.bl.uk
www.1914-1918.net
www.bbc.co.uk/guides/zts3b9q
www.biblesociety.org.uk
www.cwgc.org.uk
www.greatwar.nl
www.london-gazette.co.uk
www.longlongtrail.co.uk
www.mymethodisthistory.org.uk
www.mywesleyanmethodists.org.uk
www.nationalarchives.gov.uk
www.scarletfinders.co.uk
www.scoutsrecords.org
www.woolmerforest.org.uk

Index